Contents

Executive Summary

Higher education is one of the most important investments individuals can make for themselves and for our country. Many students access student loans to help finance their education, and last year federal student loans helped 9 million Americans to make that investment in their futures. Typically, that investment pays off, with bachelor's degree recipients earning $1 million more in their lifetime and associate's degree recipients earning $360,000 more, compared to high school graduates. Society also benefits from these investments through such mechanisms as higher tax revenues, improvements in health, higher rates of volunteering and voting, and lower levels of criminal behavior.

At the same time too many Americans feel that college may be financially out of reach and are concerned about rising student loan debt. Student loan debt can be especially burdensome for those who do not graduate or who attend schools that do not deliver a quality education. However, unmanageable debt is not the only issue facing current and former students. Some individuals who could benefit from a high quality postsecondary education do not apply and enroll in college, under-investing in education and shortchanging their future.

Multiple factors have contributed to the challenge of ensuring that all students who could benefit from a college degree are able to attend a quality school, graduate, and then repay their loans on manageable terms after they graduate. These include rising tuitions; hardship caused by the Great Recession; complexities of the labor market; variations in program quality across the college landscape; and lack of information to help students make good college choices.

The Obama Administration has taken several steps to address these challenges. To help expand college opportunity, the President has doubled investments in grant and scholarship aid through Pell grants and tax credits, provided students and their families better and more accessible information about college costs and quality through the College Scorecard, simplified the application for federal student aid, and protected students from low-quality schools. To help borrowers manage debt after college, the Administration has also created better debt repayment options like the President's Pay as You Earn (PAYE) plan, which caps monthly student loan payments at 10 percent of discretionary income.

While more work remains, we are starting to see these efforts pay off. Today, more than four out of five Direct Loan recipients with loans in repayment are current on their loans. Delinquencies, defaults, and hardship deferments are all trending downward, and nearly three million borrowers since 2010 have successfully accessed a pathway out of default through loan rehabilitation. To ensure student loans are manageable, the Administration has cut student loan interest rates, saving a typical student $1,000 over the life of loans borrowed this year. Additionally, more borrowers are making use of flexible income driven repayment plans that make it easier to successfully manage student debt after college, with nearly 5 million Direct Loan borrowers now enrolled in repayment options like the PAYE plan.

New data offer insights into the recent trends in student borrowing and repayment outcomes that build on our understanding of the overall health of the student loan portfolio, highlight areas of the student loan portfolio where Americans have benefitted from the Administration's efforts thus far, and identify key areas where there is still work to be done.

Investments in higher education—roughly 50 percent of which are at least in part financed by federal student loans—typically yield large returns. However, the return to college varies substantially across individuals, institutions, and programs.

- Over the course of a career, the median worker with a bachelor's degree earns nearly $1 million more than the same type of worker with just a high school diploma, when both work full-time, full-year from age 25. The same type of worker with an associate's degree earns a premium of about $360,000. Individuals with college degrees also see lower unemployment rates and have increased odds of moving up the economic ladder.
- While data suggest that the overall return to a college education is near historic levels, there is substantial variation across individuals. Much of this variation is related to the schools students attend and the programs they select. In particular, evidence suggests that the relatively low returns at for-profit colleges are increasingly becoming a cause for concern, especially given the high rates of borrowing by students at those schools.

As of 2015, outstanding student debt had grown to $1.3 trillion, due in large part to rising enrollments and a larger share of students borrowing. While the average loan size has also increased, the average undergraduate borrower owes $17,900 in debt.

- During the Great Recession, enrollment and federal student loan borrowing increased as more individuals, facing weak labor market prospects, decided to go to school to upgrade their skills. The largest increases occurred among lower income and older, independent students who largely attended for-profit and community colleges.
- Increases in per-borrower debt have also contributed to the expanding student loan portfolio, with average outstanding balances adjusted for inflation increasing by roughly 25 to 30 percent between fiscal years 2009 and 2015 alone. The precise causes of this increase are not yet well understood, but rising tuition and expenses, in part due to reductions in state funding for public colleges, is one factor known to be playing a role.
- Despite the increase in per-borrower debt, 59 percent of borrowers continue to owe less than $20,000 in debt; the average amount of undergraduate loans that borrowers held in 2015 was $17,900, and large-volume debt was more prevalent among graduate loans.

Many students who entered college during the recession did not receive an education that resulted in employment outcomes that allowed them to pay off the debt they incurred.

- Repayment outcomes tend to be worse among borrowers who attend for-profit or community colleges; those who are low-income or independent; those who attend part time; and, especially, those who do not complete their degrees. Many of these types of borrowers accounted for a disproportionate share of the increase in student borrowing during the Great Recession.

- Defaults are concentrated among borrowers with small-volume loans, in large part because these borrowers are less likely to have completed their degrees. Loans of less than $10,000 accounted for nearly two-thirds of all defaults for the 2011 cohort three years after entering repayment. Loans of less than $5,000 accounted for 35 percent of all defaults. Thus while there is significant public attention on high debt burdens among traditional students attending four-year institutions, default is concentrated among a different group of borrowers.

- While borrower distress has traditionally been measured using the default rate, alternative measures of loan repayment used in this report can offer advantages over traditional, default-based measures for providing information to students about a school's repayment outcomes or building loan accountability measures. For example, income based repayment plans can shield borrowers from default when their earnings are too low to make payments on their loans. This is a positive element of such repayment plans, but means that policymakers and analysts should look beyond just default measures to assess whether there are institutions where borrowers are systematically unable to repay their loans.

Income driven repayment plans like the President's PAYE plan, which caps monthly student loan payments at 10 percent of discretionary income, are benefiting nearly 5 million borrowers.

- The share of borrowers with federally managed debt who are enrolled in income driven repayment has quadrupled over the last four years from 5 percent in the first quarter of fiscal year 2012 to 20 percent in the first quarter of fiscal year 2016.

- Income driven repayment plans recognize that most students see significant income gains from their higher education, but that those gains often are small shortly after leaving school and grow significantly larger over time. Thus, these plans allow borrowers to make smaller, or even zero, payments early in their careers and adjust their payments as their earnings grow.

- Data show that income driven repayment borrowers tend to come from more disadvantaged backgrounds than borrowers on the standard repayment plan. Among borrowers with undergraduate loans enrolled in income driven repayment as of the third quarter of fiscal year 2015, the average family income was $45,000, compared to $57,000 for those on the standard repayment plan, based on the first Free Application for Federal Student Aid (FAFSA) the borrower filed.

- Income driven repayment is helping many borrowers who showed signs of distress prior to enrolling. Among borrowers who entered repayment in fiscal year 2011 and enrolled in income driven repayment, over 40 percent had defaulted, had an economic hardship deferment, or had a single forbearance of more than 2 months in length before entering their first income driven repayment plan.

- For the 2011 cohort, borrowers across all sectors had lower monthly payments in income driven repayment, despite having accumulated, on average, larger amounts of debt.

The rise in student loan debt has created challenges for some borrowers with lower earnings, but has not been a major factor in the macroeconomy.

- Despite its steady rise over the past decade, aggregate student loan debt remains small relative to aggregate income. In 2015, total student loan debt was 9 percent of aggregate income, up from 3 percent in 2003. By itself this is considerably smaller than the rise in mortgage debt prior to the crisis and it has also been accompanied by a reduction in other forms of consumer debt.
- Additional student debt, as an investment in education, is associated with additional income, putting many households in a better position to buy homes or start businesses. By age 26, households with student debt are more likely to buy a house than those that did not attend college. By age 34, college attendees with and without student debt are equally likely to buy a home, and both much more likely than those without a college education. Research studies have found that conditional on a given education, higher student debt explains, at most, a small fraction of the decline in homeownership among younger households.
- At the same time, the increase in defaults on student loans as well as the increase in high-loan balances for low earners can be real concerns at the individual level, potentially leading to compromised credit and reduced home buying for some individuals.

Introduction

The college earnings premium has reached historical levels in recent years, reflecting a trend over several decades of increasing demand for skilled workers. In 2014, the median full-time, full-year worker over age 25 with a bachelor's degree (but no higher degree) earned roughly 70 percent more than a worker with just a high school degree (CPS ASEC, CEA calculations). Moreover, people with a college degree are more likely to be employed—facing both lower unemployment rates and higher rates of labor force participation. In a global marketplace that increasingly rewards advanced skills and knowledge, higher education may be the single most important investment young people can make in their futures. For a growing number of Americans, federal student loans are an essential means to realizing the benefits of higher education. In the fall of 2013, over 20 million students enrolled in a Title IV institution (or an institution eligible for federal aid). Roughly half of these students used federal student loans to help finance their education.

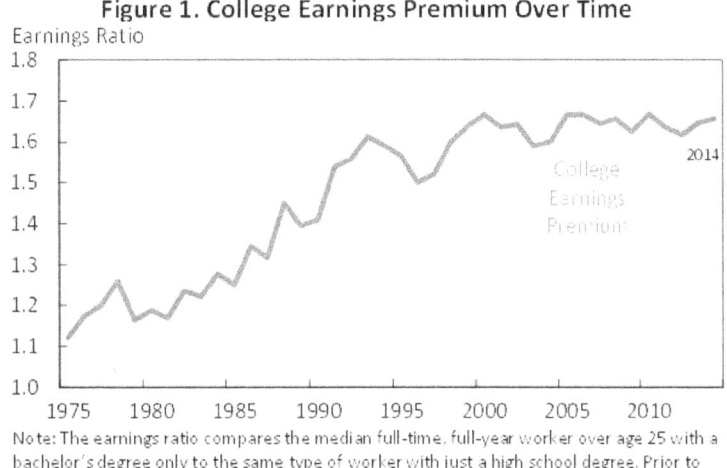

Figure 1. College Earnings Premium Over Time

Note: The earnings ratio compares the median full-time, full-year worker over age 25 with a bachelor's degree only to the same type of worker with just a high school degree. Prior to 1992, bachelor's degree is defined as four years of college.
Source: CPS ASEC

The current student loan system allows millions of individuals to make investments that typically yield large private and social returns. However, evidence suggests that some individuals invest too little in their education, while others struggle to repay the debt they incur. Rising tuitions, uncertainties of future labor market opportunities, economic hardship caused by the Great Recession, and the complexity of both the college landscape and the student aid system itself have all contributed to the challenge of ensuring that all students who could benefit from a college degree can afford to do so. The Obama Administration has taken several important steps to help address these obstacles, though more work remains.

Leveraging new data provided by the Department of Education, this report provides one of the first comprehensive reviews of the student loan portfolio to examine key trends in student debt. It also outlines the economic rationale for investing in higher education and provides a close look at how Administration policies have enhanced students' investments in their educations.

The Obama Administration continues to build on its record of progress to help ensure that all students who can benefit from a college degree are able to do so. These include: reforming student loan laws; lowering the cost of college through increases in tax credits and grant aid; spurring innovations in higher education that can reduce costs, improve quality, and drive completion through programs like the First in the World; providing timely, actionable information to students to make better college choices based on cost and value through the College Scorecard; making it easier to access critical financial aid resources through the FAFSA; connecting students to flexible and affordable repayment options to help them manage their debt and avoid the negative consequences of default; strengthening the financial aid rules to protect students from poor-performing colleges that leave students with unmanageable debt; making two years of community college free for responsible students with the President's America's College Promise plan; and calling on Congress to enact key reforms to increase college completion for Pell grant recipients.

Record of accomplishments:

- In 2010, President Obama signed student loan reform into law, generating over $60 billion in savings—redirecting that money back to students and taxpayers. In 2013, he signed into law further reforms to interest rates on student loans, lowering interest rates for nearly 11 million borrowers.

- The Administration has increased the maximum Pell Grant award by $1,000 and tied it to inflation, and on average, Pell Grants reduce the cost of college by $3,700 for 8 million students a year today. In addition, this Administration established the American Opportunity Tax Credit (AOTC), which provides a maximum credit of $2,500 per year—or up to $10,000 over four years—to expand and replace the Hope higher education credit. The bipartisan tax and budget agreement signed into law in December 2015 made the AOTC permanent. In 2016, the AOTC will cut taxes by over $1,800, on average, for nearly 10 million families.

- The Administration has encouraged greater innovation and a stronger evidence base around effective strategies to promote college success through 42 First in the World (FITW) grants that fund and test interventions at institutions across the nation, as well as through the Experimental Sites initiative that pilots reforms to existing higher education policies.

- The new College Scorecard gives students access to the most reliable and comprehensive data on students' outcomes at individual colleges, including data on former students' earnings, debt by completion status, and borrowers' repayment rates. By providing students and families with high-quality, easily understood information, the Scorecard helps students make better investment decisions that lead to higher returns.

- The Administration has made the FAFSA simpler and this fall the FAFSA will be available earlier. With these changes, families will be able to complete the FAFSA as early as October and will be able to use income information from two-year-old completed tax returns rather than waiting for more recent tax return information to be available. This will help students and their families understand the aid they will qualify for at the time students apply to colleges and reduce the complexity students face when they apply for aid, improving the information they have when making decisions about where to apply.

- The Department of Education's Gainful Employment regulation will help prevent students from making poor college decisions and taking on unmanageable debt. This regulation improves disclosures from poorly performing career college programs and removes financial aid access from programs that consistently fail accountability standards. Additionally, among other accountability measures, 2010 regulations strengthened the Department's authority to take action against institutions engaging in deceptive advertising, marketing, and sales practices and prohibited schools from compensating admissions recruiters based solely on success in securing student enrollment.

- The President's Pay As You Earn and related income driven repayment plans have allowed nearly 5 million student borrowers to cap their monthly student loan payments at 10 percent of discretionary income, to ensure their debt is manageable especially in the critical years after college.

Proposals to continue progress:

- The President's America's College Promise proposal to make community college tuition-free for responsible students would offer 9 million students the chance to earn the first half of a bachelor's degree and the knowledge or skills needed in the workforce at no cost. Since the President's announcement, over 30 states and communities launched promise programs, leveraging more than $70 million in new public and private investments supporting at least 40,000 students.
- The President's fiscal year 2017 Budget included new budget proposals to support college completion, a critical indicator of successful loan repayment, for students receiving Pell grants. Informed by recent research about what works to promote persistence and completion, two proposals increase Pell Grants for students who complete more credits or enroll year-round. A third proposal offers bonuses to colleges that successfully enroll and graduate a significant number of low-income students on time.

I.   Federal Student Aid Facilitates High-Return Investments

Because the decision to attend college entails a weighing of upfront costs and future benefits, it is useful to view this decision as an investment decision. As is true of other investments, many individuals who cannot pay for college upfront may find it worthwhile to borrow to finance their education. Yet investments in higher education also present several unique challenges that make government aid crucial to supporting optimal decisions. This section begins by presenting evidence that on average, students can expect a high return from investing in college. It then describes the challenges that students and society face in financing those investments, the role that federal student aid has played in addressing some of those challenges, and the specific issues that motivate the Administration's policies detailed later in this report.

College as an Investment

When prospective students decide whether to invest in college, economic theory suggests that they weigh the personal benefits they expect to realize against the costs they expect to incur. While some benefits like satisfaction from learning are realized immediately, a primary benefit that motivates most students is the expected gain in their future earnings (Eagan et al. 2014; Fishman 2015). Unlike the benefits of attending college which are spread out over a long period of time, most of the costs are incurred up front. These costs include the direct cost of tuition and fees, after accounting for grants and tax credits that help many students offset these costs. They also include the cost of foregone earnings during the period students are in school. From an individual's perspective, attending college makes sense whenever the present value of the benefits outweighs the present value of the costs, when both are discounted based on preferences for current outcomes versus future outcomes. For those who do not have the financial resources to pay the costs up front, student loans can allow them to finance their education and reap the positive returns. Student debt can thus be viewed as facilitating investment in one's future earnings potential.

Over a career, the median full-time, full-year worker over age 25 with a bachelor's degree earns nearly $1 million more than the same type of worker with just a high school diploma (CPS ASEC, CEA calculations). The same type of worker with an associate's degree earns about $360,000 more. The present value of these earnings premiums are also high, amounting to roughly $500,000 and $180,000 for bachelor's and associate's degrees respectively.[1] The present value of the additional lifetime earnings far exceeds the amount of debt borrowers typically accumulate upon graduation, as shown in Figure 2 below.[2] The figure suggests that the present value of added earnings is roughly 15 times the magnitude of the present value of debt. It should be noted that the present value of debt does not capture all of the costs of a college education.

---

[1] The net present value calculation here and elsewhere in the report uses a discount rate of 3.76 percent, corresponding with the current interest rate on undergraduate loans.

[2] To draw this comparison, Figure 2 uses the total debt that borrowers accumulate upon completing an associate's degree, bachelor's degree, or graduate degree from the National Postsecondary Student Aid Study (2012) converted to 2015 dollars.

In particular, it does not include tuition paid from savings, and it may not fully capture the opportunity cost of foregone earnings.[3] But even when these costs are included, the present value of added earnings typically exceeds the total cost of college by an order of magnitude (Avery and Turner 2012).

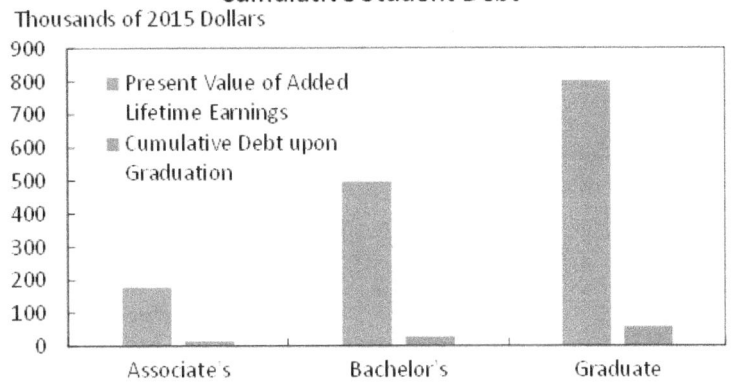

Figure 2. Present Value of Added Lifetime Earnings and Cumulative Student Debt

Thousands of 2015 Dollars

Note: Lifetime earnings are calculated by summing median annual earnings for full-time, full-year workers at every age between 25 and 64 by educational attainment, subtracting earnings for the same type of worker with only a high school degree, and converting to present value using a 3.76% discount rate.
Source: CPS ASEC 2014 and 2015; NPSAS 2012

The increase in lifetime earnings, however, is not necessarily caused by obtaining a college degree, as students who attend college may have been more skilled or more connected and thus would have earned more regardless. But the same conclusion is supported by rigorous economic research that attempts to isolate the causal effects of college attendance by comparing individuals who differ in their educational achievement but who are otherwise similar in their earnings potential. Such studies estimate that individuals who attend college earn between 5 to 15 percent more on average per year of college than they would if they had not gone to college (Kane and Rouse 1993; Card 1995; Zimmerman 2014; Ost, Pan, and Webber 2016; Turner 2015; Bahr et al. 2015; Belfield, Liu and Trimble 2014; Dadgar and Trimble 2014; Jacobson, LaLonde, and Sullivan 2005; Jepsen, Troske and Coomes 2012; Stevens, Kurlaender and Grosz 2015).

Importantly, some research also suggests that the returns to college have been just as high, if not higher, for "marginal students"—that is, students who are on the border of either attending or completing college. These students are often from low-income families and their decisions often hinge on the cost or accessibility of college. Early studies by Kane and Rouse (1993) and Card (1995) used variation in college proximity to identify the returns to college, and both found especially large returns to students for whom proximity was a decisive factor. A compelling study by Zimmerman (2014) studies variation in outcomes resulting from score cutoffs for admission at Florida International University, a four-year school with the lowest admissions standards in the Florida State University System. He finds that marginal students who gain admission experience

---

[3] The opportunity cost of college includes foregone earnings but does not include costs such as food and rent that would be incurred even if one were not in school. Some of these costs may be captured in the debt figures because students can borrow to cover the costs of living.

sizable increases in earnings compared to those who just miss the admission cutoff (and who are thus unlikely to attend any four-year college). He estimates that the earnings gains lead to meaningful returns net of costs, with even higher returns for students from lower-income families. Using a similar methodology, Ost, Pan, and Webber (2016) study the benefit of completing college at one of 13 public universities in Ohio among low-performing students whose GPAs are close to the cutoff for dismissal. They find substantial earnings benefits for those who just pass the cutoff and complete their degree. Turner (2015) similarly finds that women who attend college after receiving welfare benefits experience large and significant earnings gains if they complete credentials.

In addition to having higher earnings, college graduates are also 1.3 times more likely to work than high school graduates. Data from the Bureau of Labor Statistics show that college graduates with at least a bachelor's degrees participate in the labor force at a higher rate than high school graduates (74 vs. 57 percent in 2015)[4] and also face a lower unemployment rates among those who participate (2.6 vs. 5.4 percent in 2015). Those with some college but not a bachelor's degree are also more likely to work than high school graduates, with a labor force participation rate of 67 percent and an unemployment rate of 4.5 percent in 2015. Related to the higher earnings of college graduates and their greater propensity to work, Haskins, Isaacs, and Sawhill (2008) find that individuals with college degrees have increased odds of moving up the economic ladder. Moreover, college graduates also experience a wide range of non-economic benefits like health and happiness (Oreopoulos and Salvanes 2011). These statistics suggest that on average, college is an excellent investment for the individual.

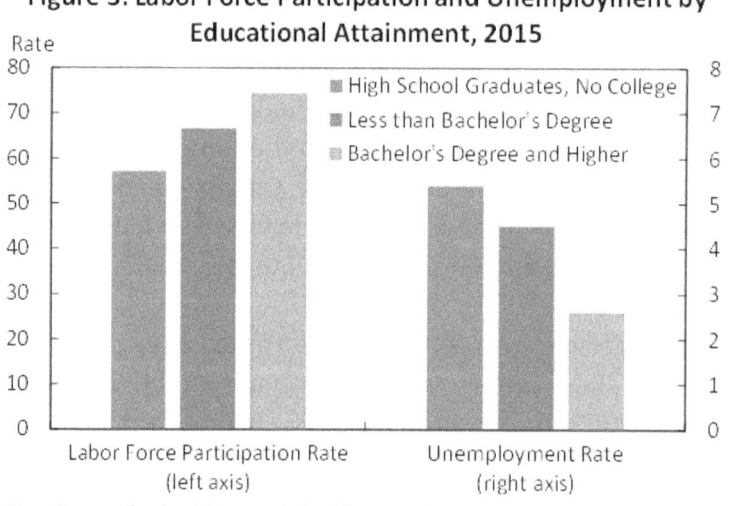

Figure 3. Labor Force Participation and Unemployment by Educational Attainment, 2015

Note: Data are for the civilian population 25 years and over.
Source: Bureau of Labor Statistics

Overall, the evidence shows that the expected returns to college are high, both for college students as a whole and for students who are most likely to be affected by policies that expand

---

[4] See CEA's 2014 and 2016 reports on labor force participation for a more detailed discussion about educational attainment and labor force participation.

college access or improve completion. Despite the fact that some borrowers experience poor outcomes, the sizeable expected returns for prospective students on the margin of attendance point to the importance of making sure that all individuals are able to optimally invest in their futures.

The Role for Federal Student Aid

Federal student aid policy offers a set of complementary tools to help individuals make educational investments that maximize the returns both to the individuals themselves and to society. Economic theory and data-driven research point to several reasons why many high-return investments would go unrealized in the absence of federal programs to support them. One reason is that college education has positive social externalities, meaning that the private benefits discussed above do not take into account the additional social benefits of college enrollment. Higher earnings mean higher tax revenue and lower government expenditure on transfer programs. Increasing education levels yields more collaboration between skilled workers, which can lift labor productivity growth where they live and work (Moretti 2004), and more education may be associated with more innovative activity through more scientists and researchers. Increased educational attainment has also been linked to higher levels of volunteering and voting and lower levels of criminal behavior (Dee 2004; Lochner and Moretti 2004).

Since college is costly, and individuals usually do not consider societal benefits when deciding whether to attend, federal programs that help to offset college costs are important for inducing socially beneficial investments. Such programs include the Pell Grant program for low-income students, the American Opportunity Tax Credit (AOTC), and subsidized loan programs that reduce the cost of borrowing. In addition, Public Service Loan Forgiveness and Teacher Loan Forgiveness help address social externalities by reducing debt burdens for individuals whose careers often provide societal benefits that exceed private benefits. The social benefits of a more educated workforce are an important motive for federal student aid.

Yet equally important is the fact that even when the private returns to college are high, the private market is usually unwilling to supply educational loans—especially to students from low-income families. A key reason for this market failure is that the knowledge, skills, and enhanced earnings potential that a student obtains from going to college cannot be offered as collateral to secure the loan. The lack of a physical asset makes educational loans very different from mortgages or car loans, which provide recourse in the form of foreclosure or repossession in cases when the borrower is unable to repay.

A major function of the federal student loan system is to ease the credit constraints caused by imperfections in the private loan market and ensure that all citizens have access to affordable loans. Although a private loan market exists, the loans typically require a co-signer. At present, the private market constitutes only a small share of student loans—in 2012, 6 percent of undergraduates used private loans to finance their education (NPSAS 2012, CEA tabulations)—and, in some cases, is generally accessible only to students with strong credit histories or high family income.[5] Additionally, private loans often do not come with the various consumer protections that federal loans have, including discharge in instances of death or permanent disability. Federal loans, on the other hand, afford all students the ability to borrow to invest in their education and help cover living costs while they are in school, while loan caps and strict discharge rules help to prevent borrowers from taking out more loans than they would reasonably be able to repay.

Economic theory suggests that without access to federal student loans, financially constrained students would be less likely to attend college; they would also be more likely to work while in school and might enroll in fewer course credits to reduce the direct costs. Recent research supports these conclusions. In a study of students enrolled at public colleges in Texas, Denning (2016) finds that increased financial aid in the form of both loans and grants reduces time spent working while in school and accelerates time to graduation. Wiederspan (2015) uses administrative records to study students impacts associated with the decision of community colleges to opt out of the Stafford loan program. He finds that when Pell-eligible community college students were offered federal loans in their financial aid package, they attempted more credits in their first year and were more likely to attempt and complete math and science classes. Likewise, Dunlop (2013) finds positive impacts of loan access at community colleges across the country. Using a separate research design based on banking deregulation in the United States from the 1970s to the 1990s, Sun and Yannelis (2015) also find that improving access to credit raises college enrollment and completion. Finally, descriptive statistics show that borrowers with greater debt typically have more education and therefore larger earnings (Looney and Yannelis 2015).

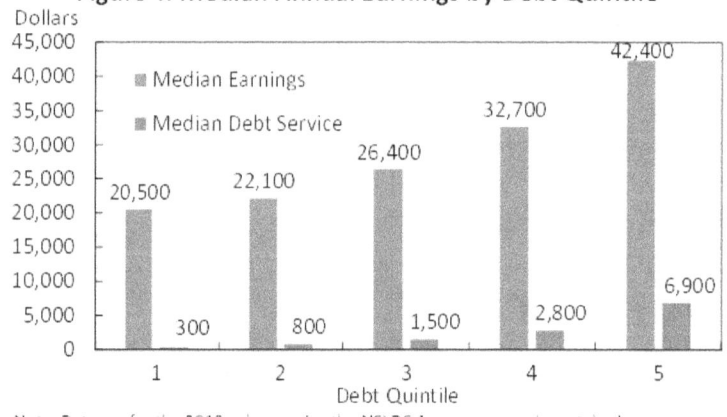

Figure 4. Median Annual Earnings by Debt Quintile

Note: Data are for the 2013 cohort, using the NSLDS 4 percent sample matched to de-identified tax records. Data are for both undergraduate and graduate borrowers. Debt service figures assume a 10 year standard repayment plan and 3.76% interest.
Source: Looney and Yannelis (2015)

While research has consistently shown that loans are crucial to helping students finance their educations, and that these investments have a high return on average, the evidence also suggests

---

[5] In the 2000s, private student loans accounted for a larger share of student loans. See CFPB (2012) for a detailed analysis about how and why the private market for student loans has changed over the last decade.

that there is still work to be done; as many individuals struggle to make optimal investment decisions. On the one hand, research shows that college enrollments have not kept up with increases in returns to college (Goldin and Katz 2008)—suggesting that overall, Americans are investing too little in higher education. At the same time, the evidence suggests that some students have accumulated too much debt, enrolling in programs that leave them poorly equipped to manage the debt they incur (Avery and Turner 2012). While the existing system helps to better align private incentives with social benefits and to alleviate credit constraints faced by potential college enrollees, several additional challenges prevent students from fully benefitting from the opportunities that the current student aid system offers. These include informational constraints and procedural complexities, which can be compounded by myopia and other psychological biases that lead to suboptimal decision making. They also include credit constraints that individuals face after they leave college and as they begin their careers.

Information Failures and Procedural Complexities

Information failures arise both from misperceptions about the costs and the benefits of college, which prevent students from making accurate cost-benefit calculations, and from uncertainty about the returns to education, which can lead to under-investment. First, research suggests that students often overestimate the costs of college. Avery and Kane (2004) study Boston public school students and find that low-income and first-generation prospective students overestimate the cost of college by as much as two or three times the actual amount. Using representative survey data, Grodsky and Jones (2007) found that on average, parents also overestimate costs, with larger errors among socioeconomically disadvantaged parents and minority parents.

In addition to cost misperceptions, research also shows that students lack information about the relationship between education and earnings (Wiswall and Zafar 2013), with some evidence suggesting that low-income students are more likely to underestimate the returns (Betts 1996). Misperceptions about the returns to college can come from both misinformation and uncertainty.

In some cases, individuals may overestimate the returns to education (Avery and Kane 2004). For example in the for-profit sector, one source of misinformation is aggressive and often deceptive marketing. A two-year investigation by the Senate Committee on Health, Education, Labor, and Pensions published in 2012 found that the 30 for-profit colleges examined spent about 30 percent more per student on marketing, advertising, recruiting, and admissions staffing than on instruction. The report also highlighted a number of tactics (consistent with a 2010 Government Accountability Office report) that misled prospective students about program costs, the availability of aid, and information about student success rates and the school's accreditation status. These tactics have prevented students from making well-informed enrollment and borrowing decisions in the for-profit sector.

Optimal decision making is also hampered by students' uncertainty about their own returns to a college education. Survey evidence shows that even students with similar backgrounds tend to vary considerably in their beliefs about the returns to education (Dominitz and Manski 1996;

Wiswall and Zafar 2013), and that many students generally view their future earnings as uncertain (Dominitz and Manski 1996). Consistent with this view, one study estimates that only 60 percent of the variability in returns to schooling is forecastable (Cunha, Heckman, and Navarro 2005). Part of this uncertainty arises from students having difficulty estimating the amount that they themselves would benefit from a college, holding college quality constant. One reason that students may struggle to estimate personal returns is that unforeseeable economic conditions can meaningfully affect the benefits students receive when they graduate (Kahn 2010; Oreopoulos, von Wachter, and Heisz 2012; Wozniak 2010). Yet another reason that students are uncertain about their returns to college is that those returns depend on the quality of the school and program of study in which they enroll, which can be hard for students to assess. Research shows that while the returns are high on average, they vary substantially depending on the type of institution students attend. A growing body of literature shows that college quality matters for completion and earnings (e.g., Bound, Lovenheim, and Turner 2010; Cohodes and Goodman 2014; Goodman, Hurwitz, and Smith 2015; Hoekstra 2009).

Research suggests that college quality varies by sector. Descriptive analysis comparing students who attended for-profit colleges to those who attended community colleges or non-selective four-year schools shows that those who attend for-profits have lower earnings on average but hold larger amounts of debt. These students are also more likely to be unemployed, to default on their loans, and to say that their education was not worth the cost (Deming, Goldin, and Katz 2012, 2013). Research that compares earnings of the same students before and after attending college—including a recent analysis of population-level data from the Department of Education along with tax data—finds that for-profit colleges offer lower returns than the returns that have been estimated for other sectors (Cellini and Turner 2016; Cellini and Chaudhary 2013; Liu and Belfield 2014). These lower returns are especially concerning in light of evidence that for-profit colleges are more expensive than community colleges, even when adding in the value of the extra government support community colleges receive (Cellini 2012). Finally, experimental evidence from resume-based audit studies further suggests that despite their relatively high cost, degrees from for-profit institutions are valued less by employers than degrees from non-selective public institutions (Deming et al. 2014; Darolia et al. 2015). But despite these poor outcomes, for-profit institutions have accounted for a large share of enrollment growth since the early 2000s, which was in part driven by funding constraints at community colleges (Deming, Goldin, and Katz 2012, 2013).

A further source of variation in returns comes from the type of programs or majors offered by a college. In recent years, a number of researchers have used state administrative data to estimate earnings gains at the program level in community colleges. Their studies have found a wide range of earnings gains, from negative figures in some programs to returns exceeding 30 percent in others (Bahr et al. 2015; Belfield, Liu and Trimble 2014; Dadgar and Trimble 2014; Jacobson, LaLonde, and Sullivan 2005; Jepsen, Troske, and Coomes 2012; Stevens, Kurlaender, and Grosz 2015; Turner 2015). Research has also shown similar variation among short degrees at non-profit and for-profit colleges, even among similar students (Lang and Weinstein 2013), although those at for-profits have relatively poor outcomes in most fields of study (Cellini and Turner 2016). A number of studies have also estimated highly variable returns by college major for bachelor's degree recipients (see Altonji, Blom, and Meghir 2012 and Avery and Turner 2012 for a review), and descriptive evidence similarly shows wide ranges of earnings post-college (Hershbein and Kearney 2014; Carnevale, Strohl, and Melton 2014). Arcidiacono, Hotz, and Kang (2012) find that students' forecast errors related to expected earnings across majors is potentially important. These findings imply that even with reasonable information about the average outcomes at an institution, differences across programs could lead to uncertainty for students when they consider their own personal returns.

To illustrate the variation in earnings that students experience after graduating, Figure 5 shows the distribution of earnings by educational attainment. For example, the figure shows that although workers with a bachelor's degree are far more likely to have greater earnings, a fraction have earnings levels more common among those with only a high school diploma. Ten percent of workers age 35 to 44 with a bachelor's degree had earnings under $20,000, compared to 25 percent of workers with only a high school diploma. This minority of college graduates may have attended a low quality college, been unable to find employment in their area of study, faced poor economic conditions, or experienced personal issues such as illness.

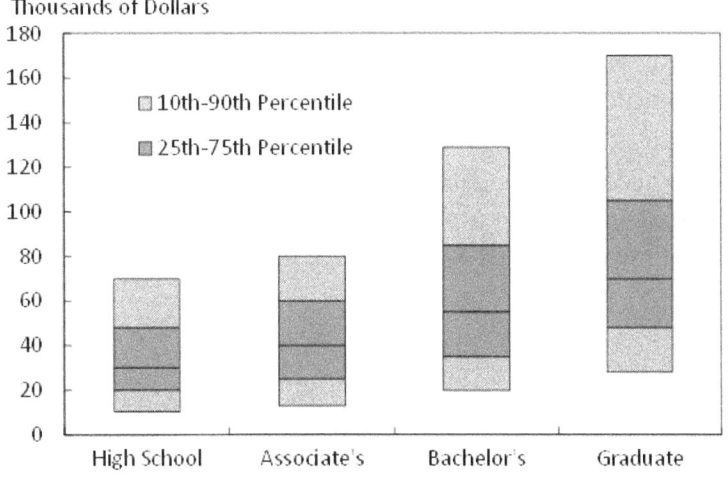

Figure 5. Variation in Earnings by Educational Attainment

Note: Data are for workers ages 35-44 with positive wage and salary income.
Source: CPS ASEC 2015, CEA calculations

The effects of poor information and large variation in earnings can be particularly detrimental since students cannot diversify their college choices. Students usually only attend one school at a time and generally focus on one or two programs. If they make a poor selection of college or major, it is often costly to switch as it can be difficult to transfer credits, possibly locking students into a low quality program. For some students, the uncertainty of returns itself may prevent them from enrolling in the first place if they are sufficiently risk-averse (Heckman, Lochner, and Todd 2006). The combination of high variability and uncertainty with limited ability to diversify means that some students will realize small or even negative returns from college even if the expected return is high.

Along with information barriers and uncertainty, complexity-related barriers may prevent students from investing properly in their education (Lavecchia, Liu, and Oreopoulos 2015). Behavioral economics shows that onerous processes can impact choices, especially when the individuals making decisions are young (Thaler and Mullainathan 2008; Casey, Jones, and Somerville 2011). Complex processes can therefore impact individuals' choices for how to invest in their education, preventing some students who would benefit from investing from doing so. Avery and Kane (2004) find some evidence that low-income students are discouraged by the procedural complexity of applying for financial aid and college admissions, even if they are qualified and enthusiastic about going to college. In their study of Boston public school students, they found that among students with at least a 3.0 grade point average, only 65 percent of those who originally intended to go to a four-year college did so. Their results are consistent with the work by Dynarski and Scott-Clayton (2006) who use lessons from tax theory and behavioral economics to show that FAFSA complexity is a serious obstacle to both efficiency and equity in the distribution of student aid. Page and Scott-Clayton (2015) calculate that 30 percent of students who would qualify for a Pell Grant fail to file the FAFSA, which is required to receive a Pell Grant. In total, an estimated 2 million students who are enrolled in college and would be eligible for a Pell Grant never applied for aid, and an unknown number failed to enroll in college because they did not know that aid was available.[6]

Importantly, experimental evidence suggests that while low-income individuals can benefit from improved information about financial aid, they may also need assistance and encouragement in order to use that information. In an experiment that provided low-income families with personalized aid eligibility information, and in some cases, assistance completing the FAFSA, only families who got additional help were more likely to see the benefits of greater financial aid and college enrollment (Bettinger et al. 2012).

Credit Constraints upon Leaving College

Finally, although the student loan system has helped to alleviate credit constraints at the time of college enrollment, the traditional standard repayment plan (that students are enrolled in by default) does not account for income volatility or dynamics once the student has left school. To be sure, many borrowers who work when they leave school earn enough to pay their student debt on the standard 10-year repayment plan. At age 25, the earnings premium seen by a typical bachelor's degree recipient working full-time and year-round is $16,000 a year (Figure 6), and this is well above the $3,500 annual payment corresponding to a typical debt amount of about $27,000.[7] Similarly, for an associate's degree, the annual earnings premium of roughly $3,000 is above the annual payment of $1,500 associated with the typical amount of about $11,000 that students borrow for this type of degree. However, because there is significant variation in the size of student loans and in the returns to college, and because borrowers may face temporary unemployment or low earnings—especially at the start of their career—some borrowers are constrained if they remain on the standard plan. In turn, the short standard repayment window

---

[6] Section VI describes steps the Administration has taken to improve the FAFSA.
[7] CPS ASEC, CEA calculations; NPSAS 2012, CEA tabulations.

may adversely affect some students' investment decisions and hinder others from successfully managing their debt.

Figure 6 helps illustrate why students may be constrained by a 10-year repayment window even if they could pay their loan in full over a longer horizon and reap a positive net benefit from their investment over their lifetime. As the figure shows, there is a strong positive relationship between age and earnings. This relationship is especially strong for those with a bachelor's degree and persists for at least 15-20 years after many students graduate from college. In short, a college investment pays off over several decades, and a 10-year repayment window forces borrowers to pay the costs at a time when only a small share of the benefits have been realized. Using discounted values for the earnings levels used in Figure 6 below, we find that less than a third of the earnings gains over a 40 year career are realized during the standard repayment window.

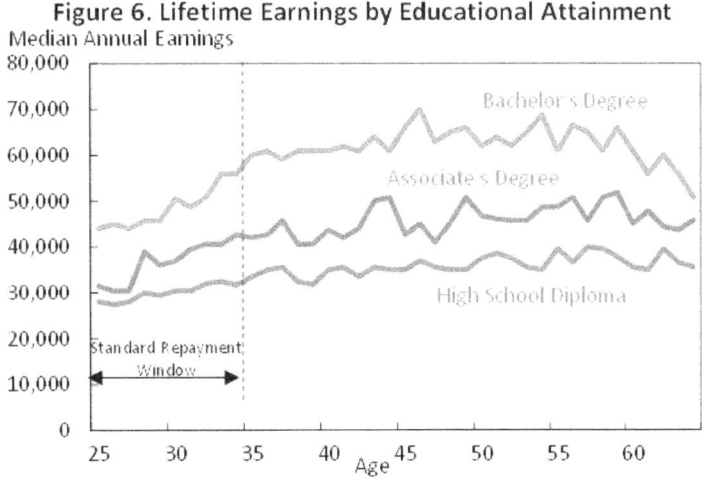

Figure 6. Lifetime Earnings by Educational Attainment

Note: Earnings are median annual earnings for full-time, full-year workers of the noted age.
Source: CPS ASEC 2014 and 2015

A short repayment window may also impose needless constraints on students who experience transitory periods of financial hardship or unforeseen economic conditions soon after leaving school. For example, research shows that college graduates entering the labor market during a recession experience sizeable income shocks and that it can take years to recover (Kahn 2010; Oreopoulos, von Wachter, and Heisz 2012; Wozniak 2010). More generally young workers are often affected more severely by recessions (Hoynes, Miller, and Schaller 2012; Forsythe 2016). A short repayment window could therefore lead to poor loan outcomes for these students despite their longer term ability to repay.

The economics literature provides some evidence that students are credit constrained even after they graduate. For example, Rothstein and Rouse (2011) show that students change their behavior in terms of early career occupational choices when they have greater debt. They examine a highly selective university that introduced a no-loans policy under which the loan component of financial aid awards was replaced with grants in the early 2000s. They find that debt causes graduates to choose substantially higher-salary jobs and reduces the probability that students choose low-paid public interest jobs, especially jobs in the education industry. The authors argue that this could be because recent graduates are unable to smooth their consumption during the early parts of their careers when their annual incomes are typically much lower than their permanent incomes. Similarly, a new study by Luo and Mongey (2016) uses longitudinal data to estimate that larger amounts of student debt cause individuals to take higher wage jobs at the expense of job satisfaction, likely due to credit constraints after graduating, reducing welfare among borrowers. However, evidence from Field (2009) based on an aid experiment at a law school suggests that aversion to the debt itself, rather than the ability to repay, may also play a role.

Overall, the evidence points to a number of factors that cause some individuals to invest too little in their educations (and in turn, to borrow too little) while causing others to borrow too much. In particular, social externalities, complexity, and credit constraints can all cause individuals to invest too little in their education. Misinformation or lack of information can lead to over- or under-investment,—or simply the wrong college choice; evidence shows that while students often over-estimate the costs of college, they may also over-estimate the benefits. Even when students have good estimates of the average returns, variation in individual returns causes some to have low returns after leaving a program, leading to trouble with loan repayment. The associated uncertainty may also cause risk-averse students to invest less than they otherwise would.

Importantly, the factors that limit access to higher education do not affect all students equally. Information barriers, complexity, and credit constraints are all more likely to affect disadvantaged individuals. Popular information channels like US News or Forbes do not contain detailed information on many of the colleges disproportionately attended by low-income students, and research shows that low-income students are less likely to accurately estimate the costs and returns to college (Avery and Kane 2004; Grodsky and Jones 2007; Horn, Chen, and Chapman 2003; Hoxby and Turner 2015). The costs of aid complexity also fall heavily on disadvantaged students, who may have fewer resources available to help them navigate the system (Dynarski and Scott-Clayton 2006), and credit constraints likewise affect those who cannot rely on personal savings, or in other words, low-income students.

In light of these obstacles, the challenges of improving the student loan system to increase its economic efficiency and fairness are clear. At the same time, there has been remarkable progress in recent years. The remainder of this report aims to provide an overview of the current student loan portfolio highlighting both the progress that has been made and the challenges that remain. Using new data from the Department of Education, it describes trends in student debt and repayment over the last five years, provides detailed breakdowns by student demographics, assesses explanations for borrowing and repayment outcomes, and explores the broader economic impacts of student debt. It concludes by describing the set of policies enacted and proposed by the Obama Administration to address challenges, help correct market failures, and improve the investment decisions and outcomes of all students who wish to invest in higher education.

II.   Recent Trends and the Current State of Student Debt

Over the past two decades, aggregate student debt levels have risen from roughly $200 billion outstanding in 1996 to a high of over $1.3 trillion dollars today (in 2015 dollars). This rise in the outstanding balance of student debt has been driven by two long-run trends: an increase in the number of borrowers and a rise in the average debt that is accumulated by each student who borrows. Underlying these long-run trends are increases in enrollment, the share of students who borrow, and the cost of college attendance. In addition to the longer-run trends, the years following the Great Recession saw a spike in student borrowing, driven largely by students attending for-profit and community colleges and by those from low-income families. As we shall see in Section IV, these types of students have had relatively poor repayment outcomes, and this recessionary expansion of debt has therefore presented new challenges to the student loan system. However, the recent data show a reversal of those short-run changes in the composition of borrowers. This section presents an analysis of these long-run and short-run trends.

Changes in the Number of Borrowers

Research finds that over the past decade, the rise in debt has been primarily driven by an increase in the sheer number of borrowers (Dynarski and Kreisman 2013). In 2004, roughly 23 million individuals held student debt (FRBNY), and this number grew to over 40 million individuals in 2015. The increase in the number of borrowers has been driven in large part by an increase in college enrollment. Enrollment reached a peak of over 21 million students in 2010, an increase of 22 percent from 2004 levels, and currently remains above 20 million (NCES 2015). While enrollment has steadily been trending upwards, it spiked during the Great Recession, as many individuals went back to school to shelter from the collapsing labor market and as the indirect cost of schooling (the cost of foregone earnings in particular) fell (Long 2015). While it is likely that population growth and the unabating high returns to college will continue to drive a long-term upward trend in enrollment and student borrowing, the past few years have seen a temporary reversal of this trend as the economy has recovered from the Great Recession. Indeed, the volume of disbursements has fallen by about 10 percent since its 2011 peak, as shown in Figure 7.

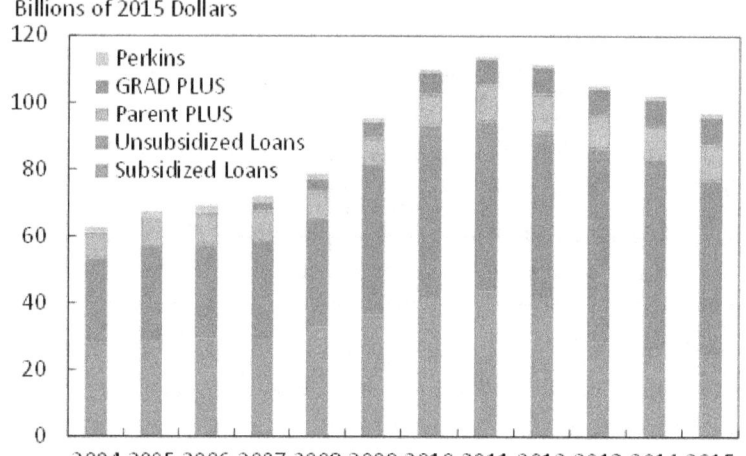

Figure 7. Student Loan Disbursements Over Time

Note: Years are award years.
Soure: Department of Education

Another contributor to the rising number of borrowers has been the increasing share of students who finance their educations with loans. Data from the National Postsecondary Student Aid Survey (NPSAS), summarized in Figure 8, show that between 2004 and 2012, the share of students borrowing increased by 10 percentage points, from 46 to 56 percent. The largest increase occurred in the public two-year sector (hereafter referred to as community colleges),[8] which saw a 14 percentage point increase in the share of students borrowing during this time period. Growth at public four-year and nonprofit colleges was more modest. In part, increases in borrowing in these sectors may have been driven by a decline in assets associated with the Great Recession or by changes in the relative availability of student loan credit compared to other types of credit (Greenstone and Looney 2013). On the other hand, over this same time period borrowing at for-profit colleges was little changed, likely due to the high baseline rate of borrowing in 2004.

---

[8] The definition of community colleges in this report may differ from other sources.

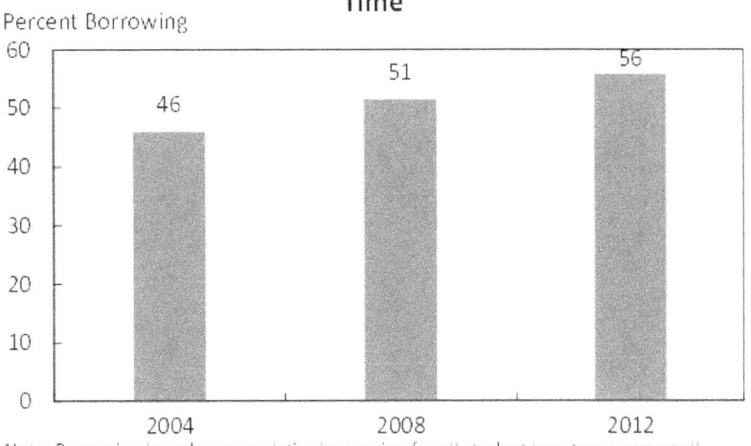

Figure 8. Share of Undergraduate Students Borrowing over Time

Note: Borrowing based on cumulative borrowing for all student loan types among all students enrolled during the given year.
Source: NPSAS 2004, 2008, 2012, CEA tabulations

Changes in the Characteristics of Borrowers and Institutions

In addition to expanding the number of borrowers, the enrollment response to the Great Recession led to compositional changes in both the types of students who borrowed and the types of institutions they attended. These changes are important for understanding not only the rise in borrowing rates but also the increases in debt per borrower and the student loan repayment outcomes discussed later in this report (Looney and Yannelis 2015).

Figure 9 shows that while the number of borrowers, especially first-time borrowers, peaked between 2010 and 2012 in all sectors, the recessionary spikes were most pronounced in the community college and for-profit sectors—both of which typically have open admissions policies. Consequently, these two sectors also experienced relatively large increases in cumulative outstanding debt. Between fiscal years 2009 and 2015, outstanding debt grew by 158 percent and 142 percent in the community college and for-profit sectors, respectively, compared to an overall increase of 107 percent in outstanding undergraduate debt. In recent years, however, the number of disbursements has declined most rapidly in these sectors.

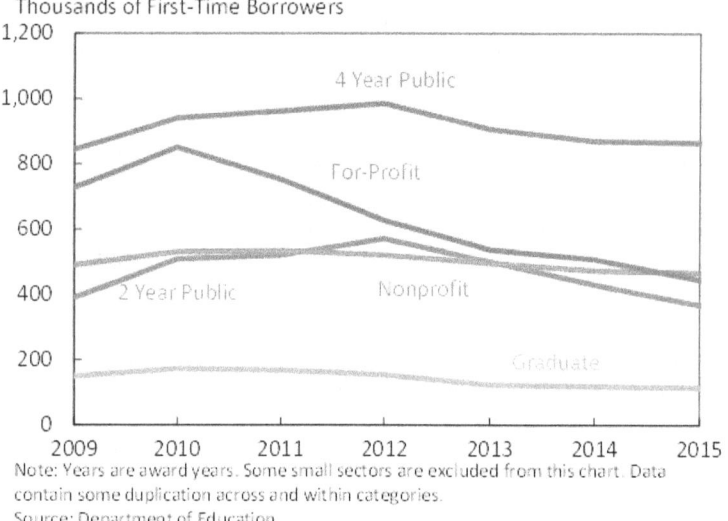

Figure 9. First-Time Borrowers by Sector

Note: Years are award years. Some small sectors are excluded from this chart. Data contain some duplication across and within categories.
Source: Department of Education

Turning to demographic trends in student borrowers, we see that the recessionary expansions and subsequent declines in disbursements were particularly prevalent among older independent borrowers and borrowers from low-income families, and these types of borrowers were more likely to attend for-profit and community colleges.[9] Figure 10 describes trends in the number of first-time undergraduate borrowers classified as independent. It shows that since 2010, the number of first-time undergraduate borrowers declined by roughly 810,000 overall, with three-quarters of this decline due to a fall in the number of independent borrowers.

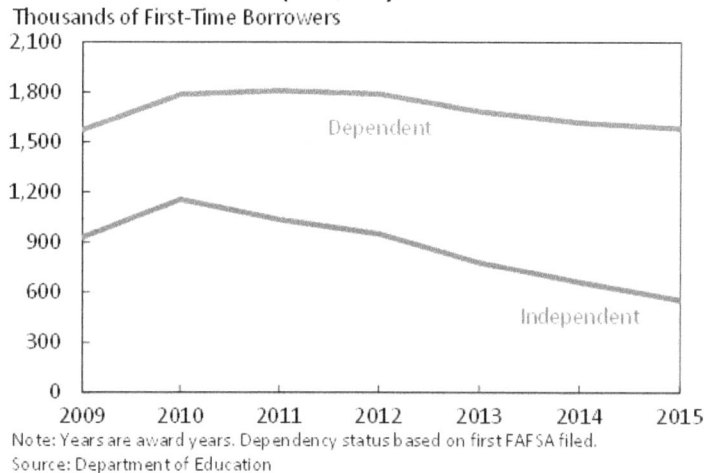

Figure 10. First-Time Undergraduate Borrowers by Dependency Status

Note: Years are award years. Dependency status based on first FAFSA filed.
Source: Department of Education

---

[9] Students are classified as independent if they are at least one of the following: age 24 years or older, married, a graduate or professional student, a veteran, a member of the armed forces, an orphan, a ward of the court, or someone with legal dependents other than a spouse, an emancipated minor or someone who is homeless or at risk of becoming homeless.

Similarly, Figure 11 shows that the number of borrowers spiked most rapidly during 2009-2011 among students from low-income families, and this group since 2011 has experienced the largest declines in the number of borrowers.[10] This decline in low-income borrowers is related to the decline in independent borrowers, as independent borrowers tend to have lower incomes, partly because their parents' income is excluded from their family income calculation. The decline in low-income borrowers accounts for three-quarters of the decline in the number of borrowers between 2011 and 2015. The rise in low-income borrowing associated with the rise in enrollment during this period could be a positive indicator of expanded college access and opportunity. However, the fact that for-profit schools accounted for much of this expansion, when combined with evidence that these schools offer relatively low average returns (see Section I above), raises concerns about the quality of the education that borrowers from low-income families received compared to the loans disbursed.

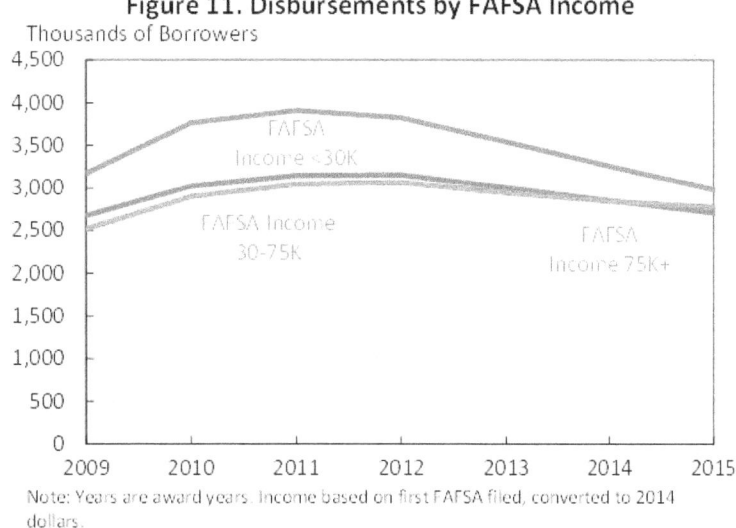

Figure 11. Disbursements by FAFSA Income

Note: Years are award years. Income based on first FAFSA filed, converted to 2014 dollars.
Source: Department of Education

Changes in the Size of Loans

In addition to a rising number of borrowers, an increase in per-student borrowing has also contributed to the rise in student loan debt. Looney and Yannelis (2015) document how per-student debt has increased over the last 30 years.[11] They show that since 2009, there has been a steady increase in the size of loans students accumulate prior to entering repayment, rising from $13,800 in fiscal year 2009 to $20,000 in fiscal year 2014 (in real 2015 dollars). Their data show

---

[10] Low-income borrowers are defined as those with family incomes of less than $30,000, based on the first FAFSA filed and converted to 2014 dollars

[11] Numbers from Looney and Yannelis (2015) do not correspond directly with the numbers noted elsewhere in the report as Looney and Yannelis (2015) use a slightly different cohort definition, focusing only on borrowers entering repayment for the first time, and a different sample of data.

that all sectors experienced increases in per-borrower debt during this time period. The recent increase in per-borrower debt represents a return to a long-run trend of growth (Figure 12).[12]

Figure 12. Median Cumulative Debt when Entering Repayment, by Repayment Cohort

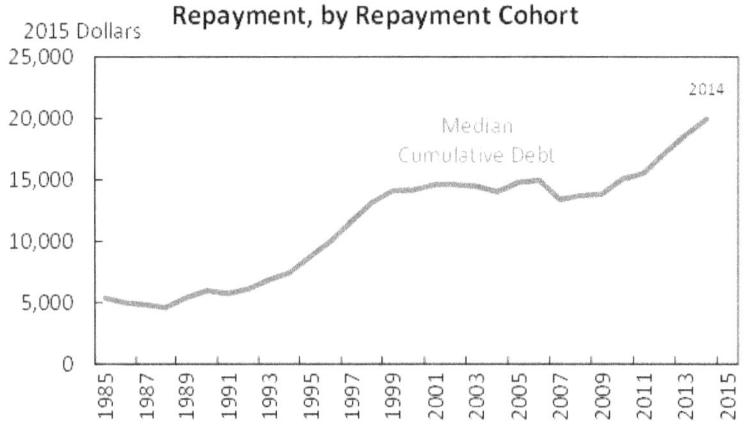

Note: Years are fiscal years. Repayment cohort contains both undergraduate and graduate borrowers entering repayment for the first time.
Source: Looney and Yannelis (2015)

Changes in College Costs over Time

The cost of college has played a smaller role in the rise of student debt.[13] At community colleges, the real increase in tuition has been modest since 2000, but the cost of room and board has increased by about $1,700 in real terms. Both tuition and room and board increased at public four-year schools, by $3,700 and $3,000 respectively. Nonprofit schools have seen the largest increase in cost, driven by higher tuition, and to a slightly lesser extent, by higher room and board. Tuition at non-profits increased by about $9,000 (or 30 percent) between academic years 2000 and 2014, while room and board increased by about $2,600 (or 23 percent).

---

[12] One reason growth flattened during the mid-2000s was temporary changes in loan consolidation policy, which allowed students to consolidate loans while they were in school. When the loans were consolidated, they entered repayment (often multiple times), artificially lowering the accumulated debt amount at repayment entry.

[13] Changes in interest rates and subsidized loan eligibility (in particular among graduate students) and the relative availability of student loan credit compared to other types of credit have also played a role but are not discussed in detail in this report.

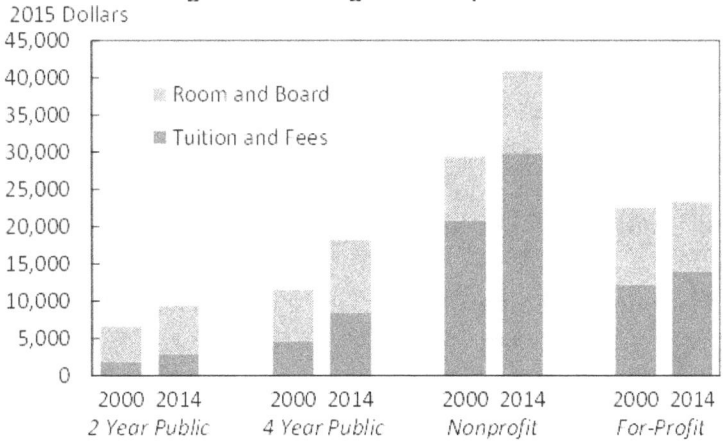

Figure 13. College Costs by Sector

Note: Years are school years, and statistics are for full-time undergraduate students. Public costs are for in-state students.
Source: NCES Digest of Education Statistics (2014)

More importantly, the net cost of college has risen more slowly. Many students receive grant aid from the state, the federal government, or the institution itself, and so do not pay the full cost of attendance. For this reason, it is important to look at the net price of college, which measures the cost that students are responsible for paying. Longitudinal data from the College Board (2015) show that while published tuition and room and board rose for community colleges, increases in grant and tax aid—in part related to increases in the maximum Pell Grant and the creation of the AOTC—offset this amount so that on average, net price stayed relatively constant. At four-year public and nonprofit colleges, aid also increased, but it only partially covered the rise in cost of attendance.

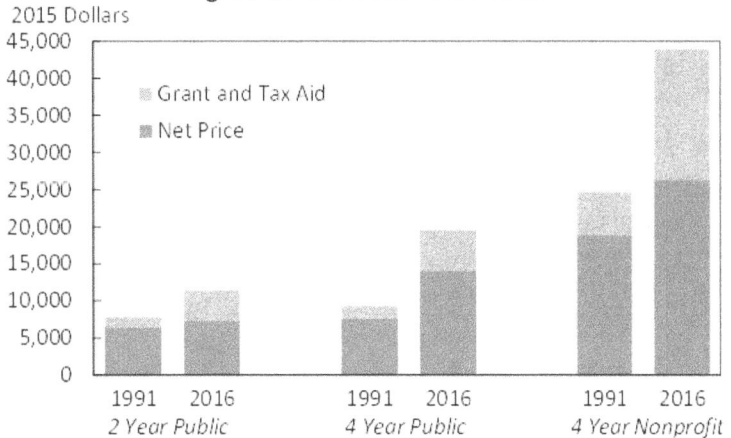

Figure 14. Net Price Over Time

Note: Years are academic years, and statistics are for undergraduate students. Public costs are for in-state students.
Source: College Board Trends in College Pricing (2015)

Reasons for the Increases in College Costs

While researchers have proposed several hypotheses about why the net price of college has been increasing, one clear contributor has been the decline in state funding. This decline was particularly sharp during the Great Recession, when falling state tax revenues coincided with rising enrollment, and it predominately affected public institutions, where roughly three-quarters of all students are enrolled. Between 2008 and 2013, state revenues per full-time equivalent student at public colleges declined from $7,400 to $6,000 (Delta Cost Project data, CEA calculations). Although revenues from federal sources increased by roughly $1,000 during this same time period, largely due to increases in Pell Grants, this did not completely offset the decline in state funding. Research shows that consistent with previous recessions, during the Great Recession, colleges increased tuition and took in a larger share of their revenue from tuition, driving cost increases for students (Mitchell, Palacios, and Leachman 2014).

Another hypothesis that has received substantial attention from researchers is the Bennett hypothesis, which proposes that increases in financial aid are captured by colleges through increases in tuition (Bennett 1987). Empirical support for this hypothesis varies by sector, with the strongest evidence found in the for-profit sector. Cellini and Goldin (2014) find that, compared with similar for-profit institutions whose students cannot apply for federal aid, for-profit institutions whose students can receive federal aid charge tuition that is 78 percent higher, capturing the majority of their students' aid. Turner (2014) also finds some evidence of capture by for-profit institutions using a discontinuity in the Pell formula to examine the impacts of federal aid on price changes, vis-a-vis reductions in institutional grant aid. However, research on the determinants of tuition at public and private non-profit schools shows mixed results, and there is currently no consensus on whether aid capture is an important phenomenon in these sectors (Curs and Dar 2010; Long 2008; Lucca, Nadault, and Shen 2015; McPherson and Schapiro 1999; Rizzo and Ehrenberg 2004; Singell and Stone 2007).

To be sure, it is likely that some schools have raised the price they charge to students to improve their quality (Griffith and Rask 2016). Hiring talented faculty, upgrading technology, and improving the resources and supports available to students all require more money, and the higher costs associated with these improvements may be justified by higher returns for students. On the other hand, some schools may be participating in an "arms race" to attract the best students by spending resources on facilities and non-academic amenities (Ehrenberg 2001), which may raise costs without contributing to student academic or long run outcomes. Similarly, some have pointed to "administrative bloat," coming from the sharp increase in non-faculty staff in recent years, as a possible contributor to rising costs, though the evidence base for this hypothesis remains thin (Desrochers and Kirshstein 2014).

III. Borrower Characteristics and Loan Size

The implications of rising average debt per borrower depend on how this debt is distributed across borrowers, and in turn, how loan size is correlated with the characteristics of borrowers and the schools they attended. In particular, rising debt levels may not lead to repayment difficulties if they are driven by quality improvements that lead to higher returns or if those with the largest loans are also the best equipped to pay them off. The evidence presented in this section shows substantial variation across individuals in the size of outstanding federal loan balances. Reassuringly, the data also suggest that the largest federal loans tend to be held by those who are likely most able to repay—including those who completed an undergraduate or graduate degree and those who attended nonprofit or four-year public institutions.

Although individual federal debt levels have been increasing and outstanding balances in excess of $40,000 are not uncommon, the amount of debt owed by the typical student remains modest. This is true especially for debt owed on undergraduate loans. As of June 2015, the majority of borrowers with outstanding undergraduate loans owed less than $20,000 on those loans, a full 42 percent owed less than $10,000, and only 10 percent owed more than $40,000. Among graduate loan borrowers, on the other hand, fully 43 percent owed more than $40,000 in graduate loans (Figure 15).

Figure 15. Graduate and Undergraduate Outstanding Loan Balance Sizes

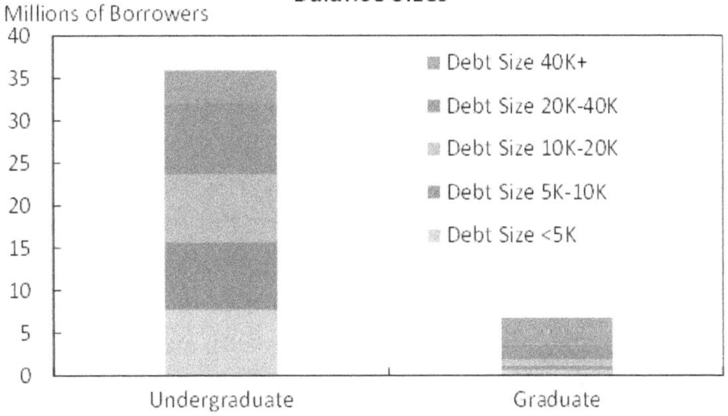

Note: Data are as of June 2015. Undergraduate and graduate are broken apart at the loan level.

Source: Department of Education

Larger loan size is often correlated with other traits that typically result in higher earnings, offering further evidence that many of those who have accumulated larger debt amounts are also better equipped to manage that debt. First, those who enter repayment having completed a degree have typically accumulated much more debt than those without degrees. Second, loan size also varies significantly across institutions; students at nonprofit institutions typically accumulate the most debt while students at community colleges accumulate the least. While completion rates and institution type are both correlated with borrower characteristics such as demographics and family income, the data suggest that borrower characteristics *per se* are not as important as these other factors in determining the amount of debt accumulated.

Figure 16 shows the amount of debt accumulated before entering repayment by demographic group and completion status. The figure shows that across a number of characteristics such as income and dependency status, differences by completion status within a demographic group are much larger than differences across demographic group within a given completion status. When viewed in light of recent research showing that completion results in significantly higher earnings, even among relatively low-performing students (Ost, Pan, and Webber 2016), the relationship between completion and debt is encouraging.

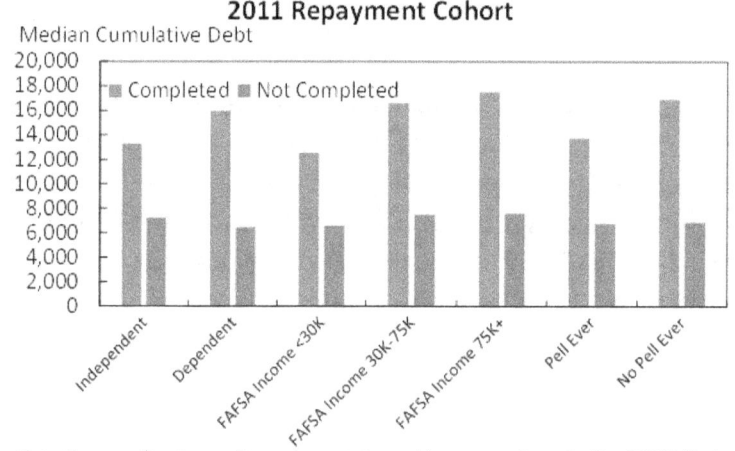

Figure 16. Cumulative Undergraduate Debt Upon Entering Repayment by Borrower Characteristic and Completion Status, 2011 Repayment Cohort

Note: Years are fiscal years. Dependency status and income are from the first FAFSA filed.
Source: Department of Education

Evidence from College Scorecard data provides some insight into the relative importance of student and institutional characteristics in determining per-borrower debt. These data suggest that much of the variation in student debt accumulation across different demographic groups can be explained by differences in the types of institutions they attend. This is illustrated in Figure 17, which plots median cumulative debt among students from high-income families against the same measure for students from low-income families at the same school. The fact that high- and low-income borrowing are roughly centered around the 45 degree line suggests that, overall, borrowers at the same school borrow similar amounts despite different background characteristics.

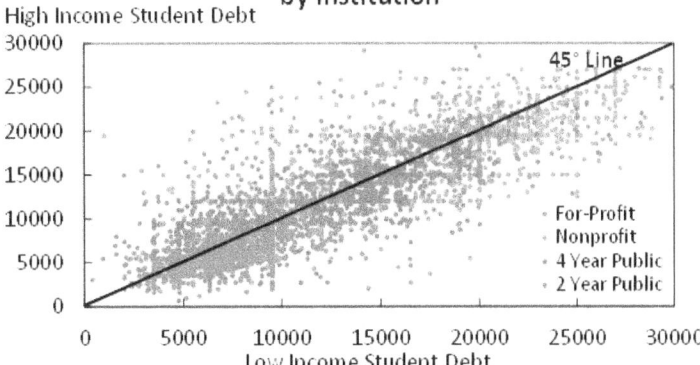

Figure 17. Distribution of Median Cumulative Debt by Income by Institution

Note: Data are for the 2013 and 2014 exit cohorts. Low income corresponds with family incomes <$30,000 and high income with >$75,000. 2 year public includes <2 year public schools for this calculation.
Source: College Scorecard

The chart also shows that borrowers at community colleges tend to borrow less than borrowers at four-year schools, with those at four-year non-profits borrowing the most. That borrowers at community colleges have relatively low debt accumulation is encouraging given that returns to two-year degrees are generally lower than returns to four-year degrees. At the same time, the chart also shows substantial variance in debt size among borrowers who attend for-profits, with median debt of more than $10,000 at many of these institutions among both high-income and low-income borrowers.

In light of research suggesting that many for-profit institutions yield low or even negative returns, especially for students who do not complete degrees (Cellini and Turner 2016), the pattern of high borrowing at many for-profits raises particular concerns about the ability of these students to repay their loans. For many borrowers, however, loan size appears well aligned with predictors of high returns, suggesting that these students should be able to repay their loans if their repayment schedules are timed to coincide with the realization of these returns. The next section examines the data on student loan repayment.

IV. Student Loan Repayment

After leaving school or dropping below half-time enrollment, students are expected to start repaying their loans, usually after a grace period of 6 months.[14]

Under select circumstances, borrowers can temporarily delay or reduce their payments by having their loans enter a status of deferment or forbearance. When students are granted deferments, they do not need to make payments, and for subsidized Stafford loans, the federal government may pay the interest on the loan during the period of deferment. Deferments can be granted for various reasons. The vast majority of deferments are for borrowers who return to school after entering repayment, but other deferments include unemployment or economic hardship (including Peace Corps service) for up to three years, or for active military duty during a war. Borrowers that do not qualify for a deferment may instead be granted a forbearance, a period of up to twelve months during which payments are reduced or stopped but interest continues accruing. Borrowers can receive forbearances for a variety of purposes, ranging from financial hardship and illness at the discretion of the loan servicer to forbearances granted for serving in a medical residency program. As the economy has improved and as the Department of Education has changed incentives for loan servicers, the share of loans in deferment and forbearance has declined.

Borrowers who do not have their payments delayed through deferment or forbearance and who have failed to make adequate payments for nine months see their loans enter default.[15] Figure 18 shows how the volume and shares of default have changed since fiscal year 2009. Although the volume of debt in default continues to rise in parallel with the overall increase in student loan volume, the share of outstanding debt in default has steadied since 2012 (Figure 19). Again, this pattern is consistent with an improving economy and the steady recovery in the share of debt that is being repaid.

---

[14]In fiscal year 2015, the majority (54 percent) of the portfolio was in repayment, up from to 40 percent in 2009, while the share of debt for borrowers in school or in grace declined, consistent with the decline in enrollment. Here and in the remainder of this section, it should be noted that Department of Education data that describe loans in repayment include loans that may be delinquent.

[15] It may take up to an additional three months for the defaulted debt to leave the loan servicer and show up in Department of Education data.

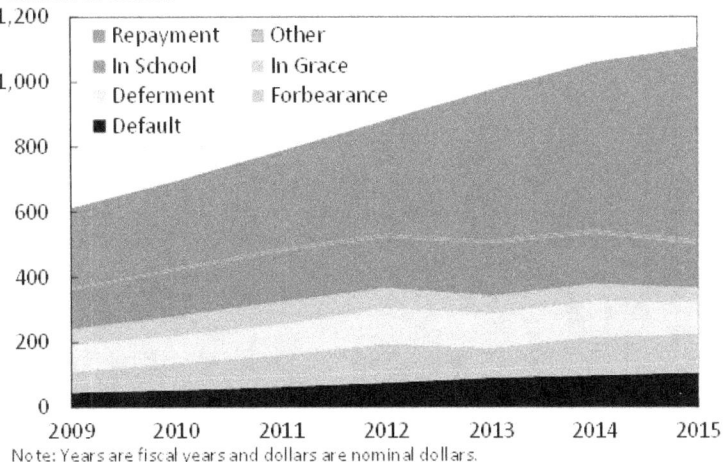

Figure 18. Volume of Outstanding Debt by Repayment Status
Billions of Dollars

Note: Years are fiscal years and dollars are nominal dollars.
Source: Department of Education

When examining defaults in the student loan portfolio, it is also important to consider that most loans that enter default remain that way in the portfolio for a significant period of time as there are limited mechanisms for loan discharge. This means that while loans that get paid off are removed from the debt portfolio, defaulted debt accumulates, raising both the share and volume of loans in default. This pattern occurs despite successful efforts by the Department of Education to collect on a reasonably high proportion of defaulted debt. For example, in the quarter ending in December 2015, the Office of Federal Student Aid's collection agencies recovered $2.2 billion in defaults (in addition to recoveries by guarantee agencies), largely by rehabilitating loans and getting borrowers on track with regular monthly payments.[16] Defaulted debt continues to accumulate for two reasons. The first is that the collection process is generally slower than the pace of new defaults. The second is that older defaulted loans that are fully repaid come from a time of lower indebtedness, while the new defaults tend to hold higher volumes. Even if new lending completely ceased, the portfolio of defaulted loans would continue to grow for many years.

Interpreting student debt default data is challenging because of the way defaulted student debt accumulates. As an example, one way data analysts often assess the health of the student loan portfolio is by examining the share of outstanding loans that are in default. However, these calculations overstate the negative loan outcomes because they include unpaid, defaulted debt from years or even decades in the past but exclude debt that was paid down. Figure 19 shows how the cumulative nature of student loan default can mask changes in repayment behavior over time. The figure shows that while the overall fraction of loans that is more than 90 days delinquent (including loans that have been in default for up to 30 years) remains elevated, the fraction of loans that are newly delinquent (having entered 90+ delinquency status within the past quarter) has declined from its peak in 2012.

---

[16] Under rehabilitation, borrowers who have defaulted can regain eligibility for new federal student aid, eliminate the loan default, and restore eligibility for benefits such as income-driven repayment and deferments. To qualify, borrowers must make nine on-time monthly payments during a period of 10 consecutive months.

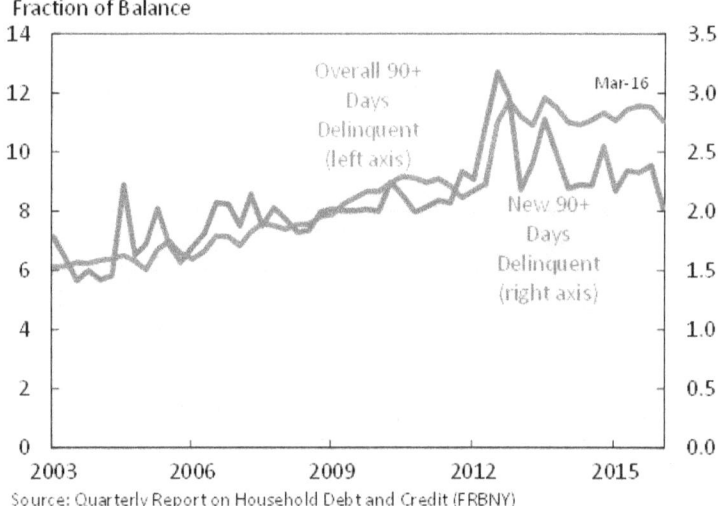

Figure 19. Student Loan Delinquency

Source: Quarterly Report on Household Debt and Credit (FRBNY)

Another challenge with data interpretation arises when analysts compare student debt default data with default data from other sectors, like credit card or mortgage debt. It is difficult to accurately compare repayment behavior across debt sectors by examining the share of the outstanding balance in default because defaulted debt in other sectors is more easily discharged with bankruptcy and does not accumulate in the aggregate in the same way as student loan debt does.[17]

Given the challenges associated with interpreting default and repayment behavior at the portfolio level, a useful alternative is to focus on repayment behavior across time at the cohort level, with the cohort being defined by when a borrower enters repayment. Figure 20 below illustrates how the distribution of loans by repayment status changes as a cohort of borrowers progresses through repayment. Focusing on the cohort of borrowers who entered repayment in fiscal year 2009, it shows the fraction of outstanding debt in each category for the first five years after entering repayment. While deferments and forbearances were common during the early years of repayment, the share of balances in these categories declined over time, corresponding to higher shares of loans that were in repayment, loans that were in default, and loans that were paid off. After five years, about 70 percent of the cohort's loan amounts borrowed prior to entering repayment were paid off or in repayment. Borrower-level data show similar trends. After five years, 17 percent of borrowers in the 2009 cohort had paid off all of their debt, and an additional 51 percent had a loan in repayment.[18]

---

[17] On the other hand, from a borrower perspective, the comparison might be more meaningful, as default in any duration impacts borrowers' credit scores.

[18] Part of the decline in deferments and forbearances in years four and five of Figure 20 is due to differences in the reporting of loan status by servicers, biasing these figures downward.

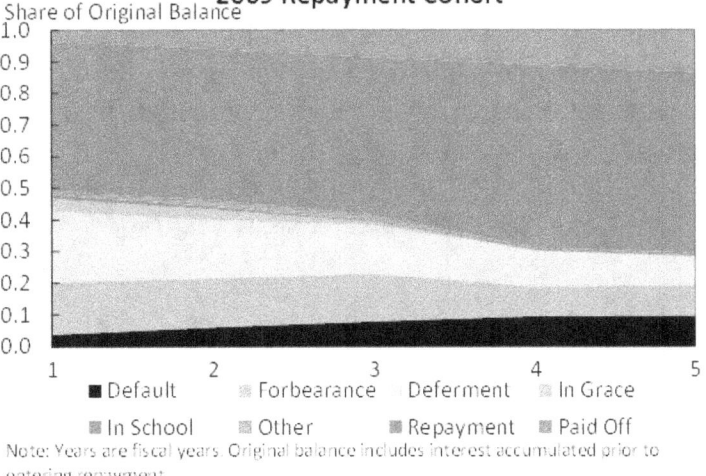

Figure 20. Loan Status by Years After Entering Repayment, 2009 Repayment Cohort

Note: Years are fiscal years. Original balance includes interest accumulated prior to entering repayment.
Source: Department of Education

Measures of Repayment Outcomes

Individual loan outcomes can be aggregated in a variety of ways to construct measures of performance. One such measure is the cohort default rate (CDR), which is calculated as the fraction of borrowers in a cohort who have entered default in the first three years after entering repayment. Every year, the Department of Education releases a CDR both at the national level and for each Title IV institution. These institutional CDRs are used to determine continued eligibility for federal financial assistance programs.[19] However, the CDR has some well-documented weaknesses which we detail in this section. We present two alternative measures to the CDR that offer certain improvements over the CDR for the purposes of reporting and accountability. The first is the "$1 down" non-repayment rate, which measures the fraction of borrowers who have failed to pay down at least $1 of their original balance, and the second is the "cohort remaining balance outstanding" (CRBO), which measures the fraction of a cohort's collective original balance that remains. This section describes these aggregate repayment measures in more detail and explains the advantages and disadvantages of each.

Cohort Default Rate

Because the CDR has been published since 1987, it is useful for understanding historical trends. Figure 21 shows how final CDRs have changed over time since 2000. CDRs began increasing prior to the recession, driven by a variety of factors—including a change in loan consolidation policy, the type of borrowers who entered repayment during this time period, and the quality of schools they attended—and continued to worsen during the harsh economic conditions associated with the recession. As described in Sections I and II, much of the enrollment increase during this time was driven by older and lower income students largely attending for-profit and community

---

[19] If loans have three-year cohort default rates that exceed 30% for three consecutive years or the cohort default rate exceeds 40% in a single year, the institution loses its ability to receive federal aid for the following three years. Certain appeals are available to schools.

colleges, which have large variation in quality. As a result, many of the students who attended these institutions may not have received an education that equipped them to find well-paying jobs and manage the debt they incurred, even if that debt was relatively small. Moreover, because many of these students were older or had lower incomes, they were less able to rely on their parents or their personal savings to help make payments.[20] In more recent years, as the labor market has improved, CDRs have begun to decline.

Figure 21. Cohort Default Rates Over Time

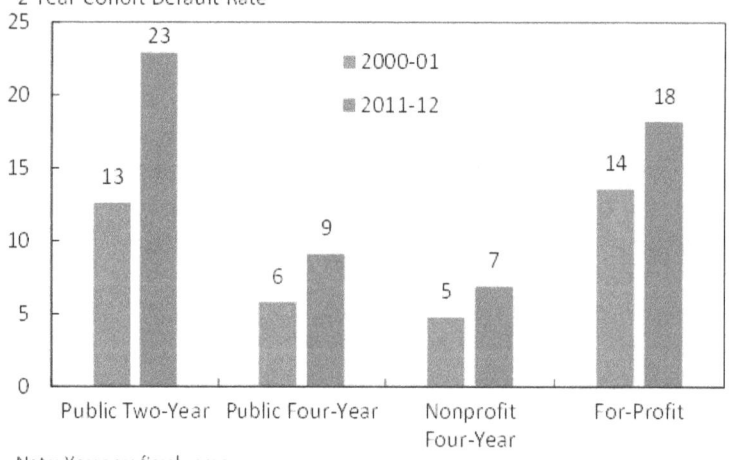

Note: Solid lines represent official rates while dashed lines are estimates by the Department of Education. Through the fiscal year 2008, official cohort default rates were measured after two years, after which they were measured after three years; during the transition period, estimates for both time periods were provided.
Source: Department of Education

Figure 22. Cohort Default Rate Levels by Sector over Time
2 Year Cohort Default Rate

Note: Years are fiscal years.
Source: College Board Trends in Student Aid (2015)

One weakness of the CDR is that it does not include borrowers who may utilize deferments or forbearances when under financial duress in the numerator of its calculation. While this protects schools against poor CDRs if their former students have temporary instances of bad luck, it does allow some schools whose students regularly receive deferments and forbearances due to poor

---

[20] The latter half of this section further details how institution and student characteristics are correlated with repayment.

economic outcomes—and who therefore may be financially unable to repay their loans—to have lower default rates than would otherwise be calculated (TICAS 2012). Additionally, as noted above, because it takes 9 months of failed payments before borrowers are placed in default and often another 3 months before the default is reported, this measure can miss early warning signs. Prior to 2009, CDRs were measured after only two years of entering repayment, making them even more susceptible to missing poor loan outcomes.

Alternative Measures

The institutional repayment rate introduced with the College Scorecard can serve as an alternative to the CDR. This repayment rate measures the fraction of borrowers who have failed to pay down at least $1 of their original balance by a given point in time after entering repayment. This measure has two advantages over the CDR. First, it better captures relatively short-term outcomes for those schools whose students regularly experience poor outcomes and are placed in deferment or forbearance. Second, it has a simple formula for identifying students who have especially unfavorable loan outcomes without needing to wait an extra year for a default to be recorded. One disadvantage with this measure is that some students enrolled in income driven repayment plans may have very low (or even zero) monthly payments, and the presence of such students could negatively impact this repayment metric even if they made payments on time. At the same time, this feature can serve as a useful indicator for poor outcomes from a school if a large fraction of students have payments set to zero for a prolonged period of time due to inadequate labor market outcomes, or have a large share of students who are delinquent on their loans.

Another informative measure, the cohort remaining balance outstanding (CRBO), uses, for all students from an institution who enter repayment at a given time, the fraction of the collective original balance that remains after a certain period of time. While this type of measure may be more difficult for borrowers to understand, it can prove useful in certain accountability schemes, as schools are rewarded for enabling students to repay their loans to the best of their abilities rather than to simply cross a threshold of default or of paying down a dollar of their loans. An advantage of the CRBO measure is that it provides a fuller picture of whether borrowers are paying down their debt in a timely manner, as opposed to making only $1 of progress. Normally, loans with a fixed monthly payment and interest rate have a predictable share of principal remaining at each point in repayment, and this metric adapts that concept to the institutional level. One key disadvantage is that the CRBO measure is much more susceptible to the types of repayment plans that students are enrolled in if it is measured relatively soon after borrowers enter repayment; all plans with extended terms will necessarily have a lower fraction of principal paid, even if the loan repayment is on track.[21]

---

[21] Only roughly half of borrowers with federally managed debt were in a standard 10-year repayment plan as of the first quarter of fiscal year 2016. Relatedly, today, the CRBO shows that repayment tends to be lower than that expected under the standard repayment plan. For example, although under the standard repayment plan, one would expect only 70 percent of the balance to remain after three years, for the 2009 cohort, 86 percent of the original balance remained.

Figure 23 shows how the three performance measures compare over time for the cohort that entered repayment in fiscal year 2009. The Figure shows that at the same time that defaults increased from 6 percent to 22 percent, the share of borrowers who had failed to pay down at least a dollar of their initial balance decreased from 52 percent to 39 percent, and the remaining loan balance dropped from 92 percent of the original balance to 84 percent. The figure highlights that, while defaults tend to rise over time, alternative measures of repayment show improvement. This discrepancy occurs because while some borrowers experience increased difficulty in repayment and are no longer able to use deferments and forbearances to ease their debt burdens, the majority of borrowers make progress in paying back their loans after five years, as measured by the $1 down metric. Additionally, the figure shows that dollar based measures like the CRBO move differently because they weight by loan size. Although schools with high rates of default tend to also have high rates of non-repayment and smaller shares of the original loan balance paid off, the figure shows how the aggregation of these measures provide different insights about repayment.

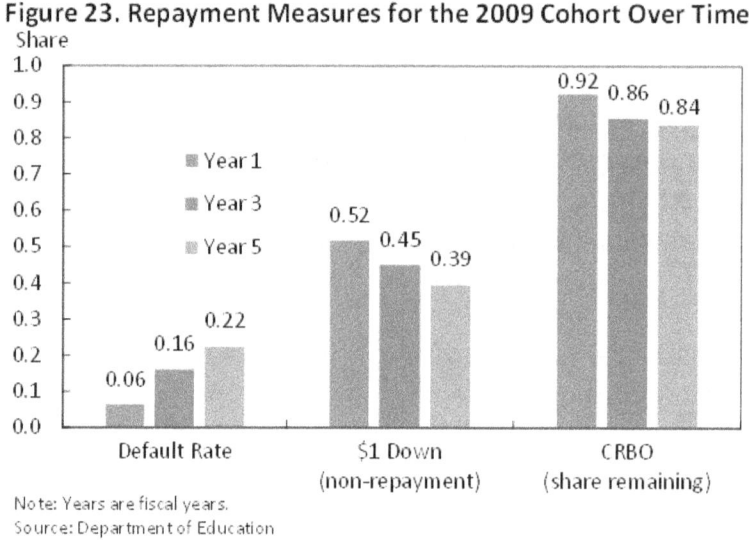

Figure 23. Repayment Measures for the 2009 Cohort Over Time

Note: Years are fiscal years.
Source: Department of Education

Lastly, a final repayment measure could take a similar approach as the cohort default rate, but capture a wider range of poor outcomes to create a better measure of students who are in good standing.[22] For example, we use Department of Education data to construct a measure that includes the share of borrowers without a loan in default, forbearance, economic hardship deferment, or unemployment deferment to define the share of borrowers in a cohort who are good standing after a period of time. These data show similar trends as the other measures described above, except that they are not affected by enrollment in income driven repayment or deferments unrelated to economic hardship. Some drawbacks to the good standing measure include that it may be more difficult to understand, that it requires better data on delinquency to truly measure good standing, and that it fails to capture systematically poor income driven

---

[22] Another measure to consider is a debt service to earnings ratio, which roughly measures the ability of students to repay—though a more precise measure would focus on discretionary income—rather than actual repayment outcomes. For a more detailed analysis of this measure, see Looney and Yannelis (2015).

repayment outcomes. For these reasons, the remainder of this report focuses on the first three measures described above (default rates, $1 down measure, and CRBO), but readers should note that a good standing measure may be appropriate to use in certain accountability scenarios or loan portfolio metrics as well. Additionally, the measures focused on below can be improved by including some of beneficial features in the good standing measure. For example, they could exclude borrowers who are still enrolled in school, along with those borrowers in military deferment or with a permanent disability discharge, as used in published Scorecard data and the proposed Borrower Defense disclosure.

Correlates of Repayment

This section examines the factors that are associated with repayment outcomes of borrowers. It is important to understand which types of students are having difficulty with repayment for two main reasons. First, good information about the correlates of repayment outcomes is crucial for guiding policy to improve repayment outcomes among existing and future borrowers. The final section of this report describes policies that the Administration has taken to improve the federal financial aid system, targeting beneficial policies toward borrowers for whom the policies will be most effective. Second, as discussed earlier in this report, the temporary expansion and subsequent decline in college enrollment during and after the Great Recession were driven disproportionally by certain types of borrowers. In particular, the share of new borrowers attending for-profit and community colleges, coming from low-income backgrounds, or having an independent status all spiked just after the recession and have declined over the five years since. Better understanding how this change in enrollment may have affected repayment in later years helps to inform policy and improve repayment outcomes.

The remainder of this section describes how repayment outcomes are related to characteristics of borrowers, their families, and their educational choices. Repayment measures are shown to be better among borrowers with higher earnings, and relatedly, among borrowers who completed their degrees, those who attended a nonprofit or four-year public institution, those who majored in a STEM field, and those who attended full-time. Borrowers from higher-income families and those who are dependents also have better repayment outcomes. Somewhat counterintuitively, because these characteristics are associated with larger amounts of debt, repayment outcomes are better among borrowers who owe more.

Repayment and Earnings

Two key correlates of repayment are the earnings of students after they leave college and, relatedly, students' completion status. Descriptive statistics also show that individuals who have completed college or who have higher earnings are more likely to experience positive loan repayment outcomes. As described in CEA's 2015 report "Using Federal Data to Measure and Improve the Performance of U.S. Institutions of Higher Education," Scorecard data show that institutions with higher post-college earnings also have better repayment outcomes, as do four-year institutions with higher completion rates (Figure 24). Descriptive data by college major similarly show that students who study fields with higher earnings after graduation, like STEM fields, also tend to see better repayment outcomes (Figure 25). Despite having similar family incomes and accumulated debt amounts while in college, STEM majors tend to earn more and are less likely to have a delinquent loan than non-STEM majors after graduating.[23]

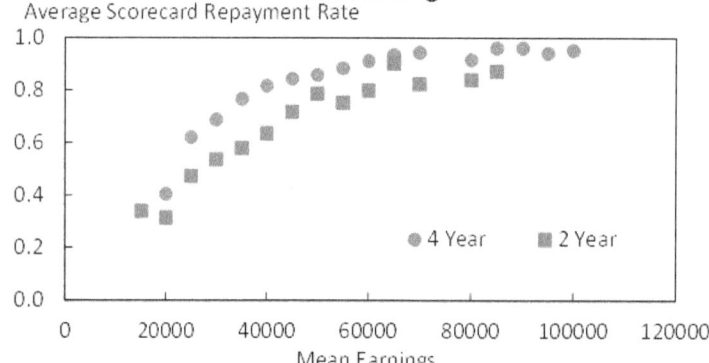

Figure 24. Relationship Between Scorecard Repayment Rate and Earnings

Note: Chart compares the 3 year repayment rates for the 2010-2011 pooled cohort to the 10 year earnings for the 2002 cohort. Outliers and bins with small numbers of schools are excluded.
Source: College Scorecard

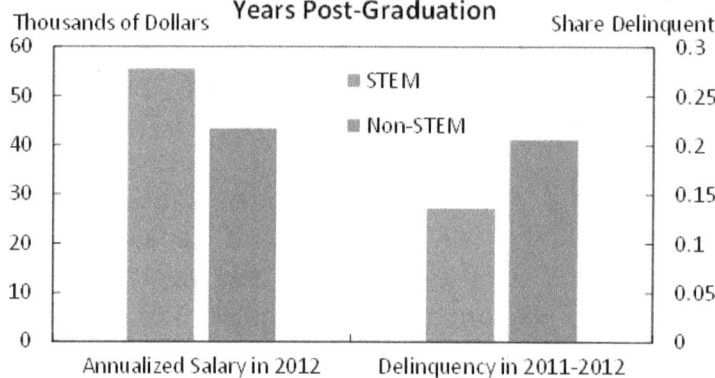

Figure 25. Earnings and Delinquency by College Major, Four Years Post-Graduation

Note: Data are for borrowers receiving their bachelor's degree in 2007-2008. STEM fields include computer and information sciences, engineering and engineering technology, biological and physical science, science technology, math, and health care fields.
Source: Baccalaureate and Beyond Longitudinal Study

In addition to simple correlations, economic research confirms that former students who have higher earnings are more likely to have positive repayment outcomes, controlling for other factors. Looney and Yannelis (2015) use a sample of all federal loans to decompose the determinants of default into institutional characteristics of selectivity and sector, dependency status, family income prior to entering college, dependency status, age, and marital status, along

---

[23] Data use the Baccalaureate and Beyond Longitudinal Study for borrowers receiving their bachelor's degree in 2007-2008 followed for four years. STEM fields include computer and information sciences, engineering and engineering technology, biological and physical science, science technology, math, and health care fields.

with variables related to post-college earnings and completion. They find that earnings and completion have a statistically significant relationship to repayment behavior even after controlling for other factors. Using a different dataset that combines credit bureau, National Student Clearinghouse, and federal data sources to study the predictors of repayment, Mezza and Sommer (2015) also find that completion is an important predictor of repayment outcomes.

Repayment and Completion

Department of Education data show stark disparities in repayment by completion status as well.[24] Among undergraduate borrowers (hereafter defined as borrowers who did not have graduate loans) who entered repayment in fiscal year 2011, non-completers had default rates of 25 percent after three years, compared with just 9 percent among completers. Differences by completion status were also large among other measures of repayment. For example, after three years, 58 percent of completers had paid back at least a dollar of their loans, contributing to a 14 percent decline in their original balance. In contrast, only 39 percent of non-completers had paid down a dollar of their initial balance and 94 percent of their original balance remained unpaid after three years.

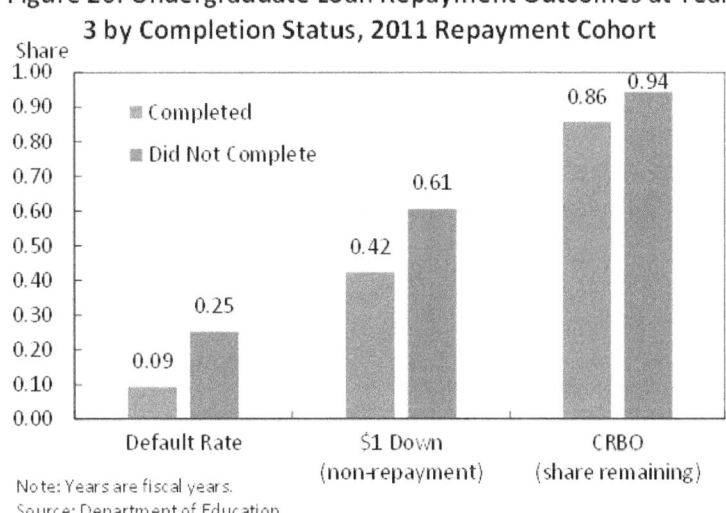

Figure 26. Undergraduate Loan Repayment Outcomes at Year 3 by Completion Status, 2011 Repayment Cohort

Note: Years are fiscal years.
Source: Department of Education

Repayment and Debt Size

Because borrowers with greater debt amounts are more likely to complete their degrees and have higher earnings after college (see Figures 16 and 4 earlier in this report), a related but counterintuitive correlate with good repayment outcomes is actually a greater initial loan amount. Defaults are much more common among borrowers with *smaller* principal loan balances. Figure 27 shows three-year default rates by loan size for borrowers who entered repayment in fiscal year 2011. Roughly a quarter of borrowers with initial debt of less than $5,000

---

[24] Borrowers who have completed any post-secondary degree, as reported in the student loan data, are considered to be completers. When showing repayment outcomes by completion status, we exclude students with graduate loans.

defaulted within three years, while only 7 percent of those with more than $40,000 of initial debt had defaulted over the same time period. The higher likelihood of default combined with greater numbers of borrowers with small loans means that loans of less than $10,000 accounted for nearly two-thirds of all defaults.

Figure 27. Share of Borrowers Who Default by Year 3 by Loan Size, 2011 Repayment Cohort

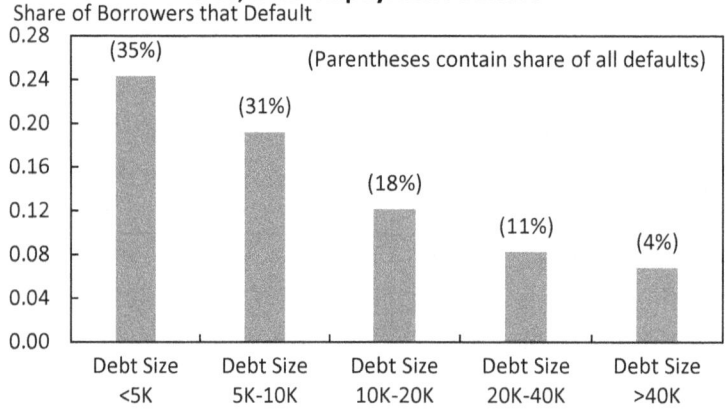

Note: Years are fiscal years. Loan size is based on balance of loan when entering repayment.
Source: Department of Education

Part of this trend is driven by the prevalence of graduate students among borrowers with higher volume loans. At any loan size, graduate students are much less likely to default, likely in part because individuals with graduate degrees have higher earnings (Figure 28). However, even when focusing on borrowers with only undergraduate loans, it remains true that small volume borrowers are more likely to default.

Figure 28. Share of Borrowers Who Default by Year 3 by Loan Size and Graduate Status, 2011 Repayment Cohort

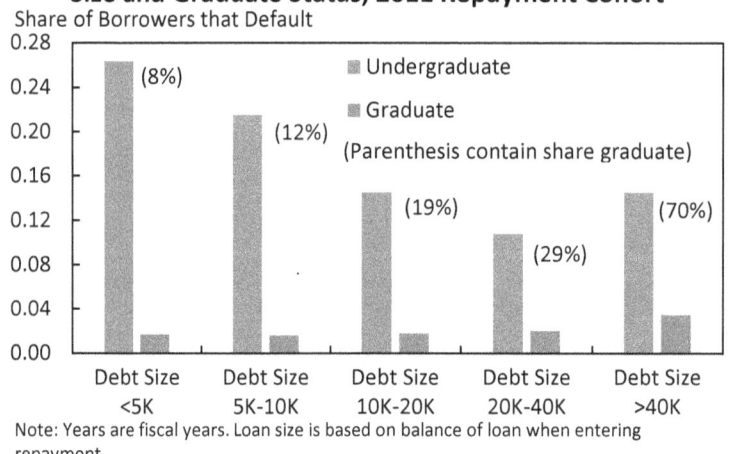

Note: Years are fiscal years. Loan size is based on balance of loan when entering repayment.
Source: Department of Education

Focusing on undergraduate-only borrowers, Figure 29 more clearly shows the relationship between completion, debt size, and repayment. The figure shows that defaults are far less common among completers regardless of debt size, but borrowers with larger amounts of initial debt are much more likely to have completed. For example, undergraduate borrowers who graduated with less than $5,000 in debt have similar likelihoods of defaulting as those who graduated with larger amounts of debt. However, fewer than 1 in 6 undergraduate borrowers with only $5,000 of initial debt completed college, compared to nearly 2 in 3 borrowers with over $20,000 in debt.

Figure 29. Relationship Between Undergraduate Default and Debt Size by Completion Status, 2011 Repayment Cohort

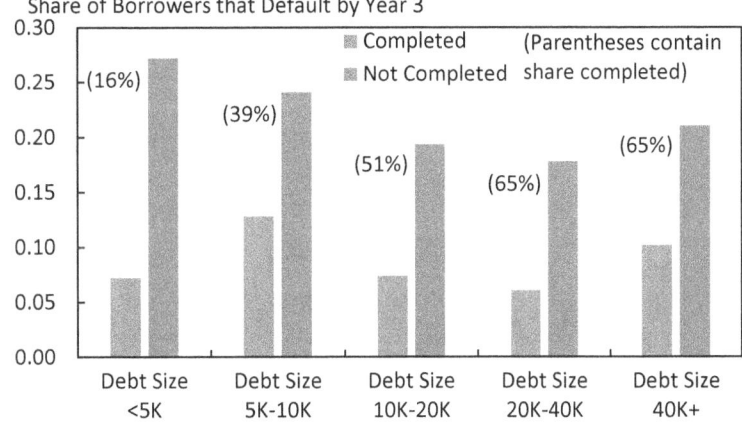

Note: Years are fiscal years. Loan size is based on balance of loan when entering repayment.
Source: Department of Education

Repayment and College Sector

Another factor related to repayment is the sector of college attended. As shown earlier for CDRs (Figure 22), loan repayment outcomes differ substantially by college sector. This relationship is present in alternative measures of repayment as well. For example, Figure 30 shows that after three years, borrowers from nonprofit and four-year public schools have paid down 15 percent of their original balance on the whole, compared with only 8 percent and 3 percent at community colleges and for-profits, respectively. Although loan repayment outcomes are similar at community colleges and for-profits, for-profit colleges present a unique challenge, as a far larger share of students who attend them borrow to finance their education.

43

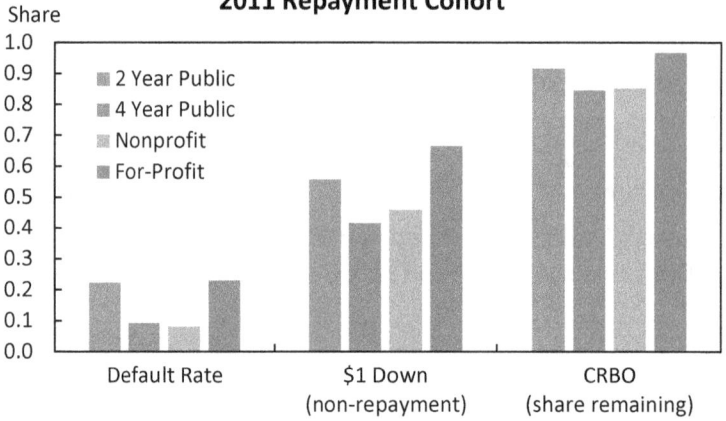

Figure 30. Loan Repayment Outcomes after 3 Years by Sector, 2011 Repayment Cohort

Note: Years are fiscal years. Some small sectors are excluded from this chart. Data contain some dupliction across and within categories.
Source: Department of Education

Although Figure 30 above shows that average repayment outcomes are relatively poor among borrowers at both community colleges and for-profit institutions, outcomes in these two sectors look less similar when we compare borrowers with the same completion status. Figure 31 shows that among both completers and those who did not complete, borrowers who attended for-profits are more likely to default. The poor average outcomes at community colleges are thus driven by the fact that completion rates are much lower at these schools.

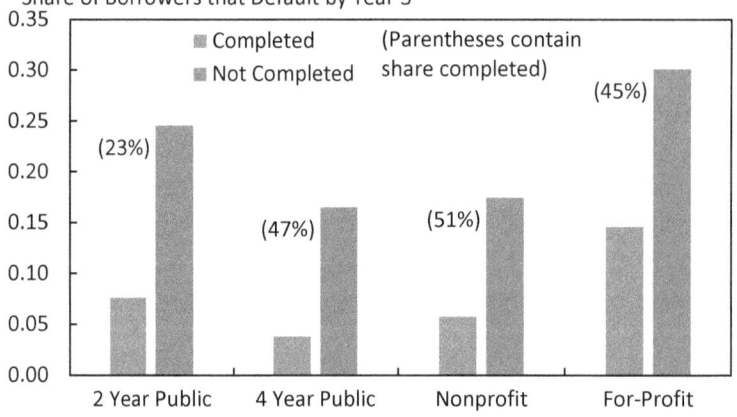

Figure 31. Relationship Between Undergraduate Default and Sector by Completion Status, 2011 Repayment Cohort

Note: Years are fiscal years. Some small sectors are excluded from this chart. Data contain some duplication across and within categories.
Source: Department of Education

Repayment and Borrower Characteristics

Repayment outcomes also differ by borrower characteristics. First, borrowers from low-income families typically have more difficulty repaying their loans, regardless of measure examined. Figure 32 below charts undergraduate repayment by groupings of family income listed on the first FAFSA. Twenty-nine percent of borrowers in the top family income category of $75,000 and above had failed to pay down at least a dollar of their initial balance after 3 years, compared to 65 percent of borrowers with family incomes less than $30,000. Among those with reported incomes, borrowers with family incomes less than $30,000 accounted for roughly 70 percent of defaults, despite making up only about 50 percent of borrowers. These differences highlight the fact that low-income students face unique challenges with repayment and need additional supports from colleges and other stakeholders to improve repayment outcomes.

Figure 32. Undergraduate Loan Repayment Outcomes after 3 Years by Income, 2011 Repayment Cohort

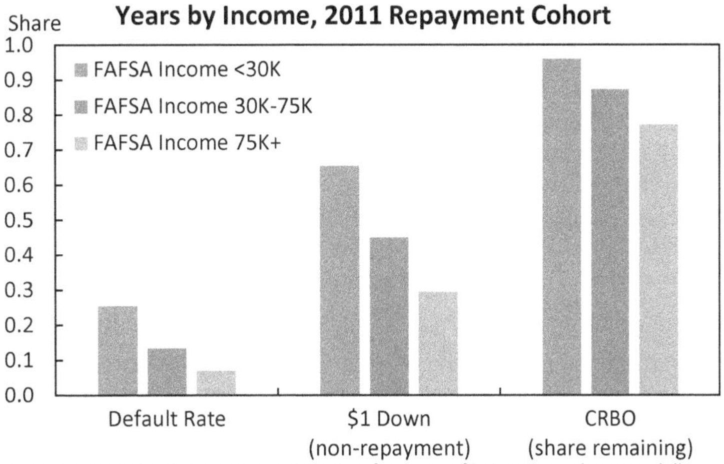

Note: Years are fiscal years. Income based on first FAFSA filed, converted to 2014 dollars.
Source: Department of Education

There are several explanations that could account for lower repayment rates among lower income borrowers. Low-income borrowers have lower completion rates, leading to poorer repayment outcomes. They may also be less likely to be able to draw on family resources to repay if they suffer an unexpected financial shock during repayment. Looney and Yannelis (2015) find that family income is a statistically significant determinant of default even when controlling for institution type, degree attainment, post-college earnings, and a handful of other individual characteristics, though the magnitude of the effect is relatively small compared to institutional measures.

Figure 33. Relationship Between Undergraduate Default and FAFSA Income by Completion Status, 2011 Repayment Cohort

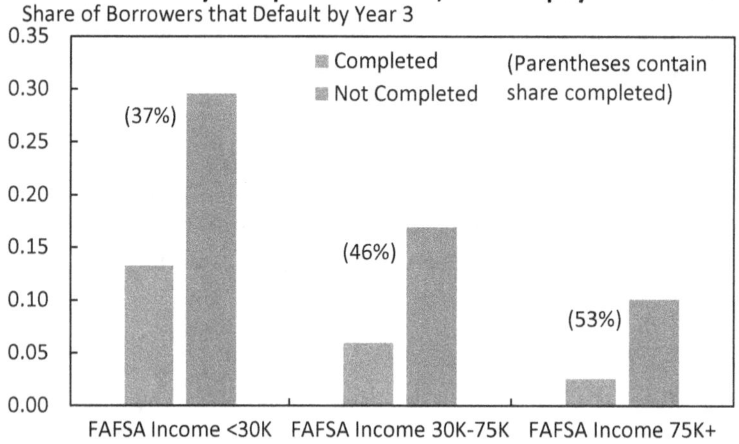

Share of Borrowers that Default by Year 3

Note: Years are fiscal years. Income based on first FAFSA filed, converted to 2014 dollars.
Source: Department of Education

Unsurprisingly, similar disparities exist when comparing undergraduate borrowers who had ever received Pell Grants to those who did not, as Pell Grants are given to low-income students. For example, 23 percent of Pell borrowers in the 2011 repayment cohort had defaulted within three years, compared to only 9 percent of borrowers who had never received Pell Grants. Likewise, undergraduate borrowers who had received Pell had in total only paid down 6 percent of their original balance by year three, compared to 22 percent for borrowers who never received Pell. Like low-income students in general, borrowers with Pell Grants may require unique supports to make sure they leave college well equipped to pay their loans.

Repayment is also associated with students' dependency status, in a pattern consistent with the relationship between this variable and other institutional and individual characteristics. At year three for the 2011 repayment cohort, undergraduate borrowers who were classified as independent when they first filed their FAFSAs had paid down only 4 percent of their loans, compared to 16 percent for dependent borrowers. Independent borrowers also had higher default rates of 24 percent, compared to 14 percent among dependent borrowers, and they were less likely to have paid down a dollar of their loans.

Repayment and Enrollment Intensity

Enrollment intensity is related to repayment outcomes as well. For example, undergraduate borrowers who had attended college exclusively part-time had a 23 percent default rate three years after entering repayment for the 2011 cohort. This differed from full-time students who had a default rate of 18 percent. Borrowers who attended part-time only were also 8 percentage points less likely to have paid down a dollar of their loans and overall had 6 percentage points more of their balance outstanding after three years.

46

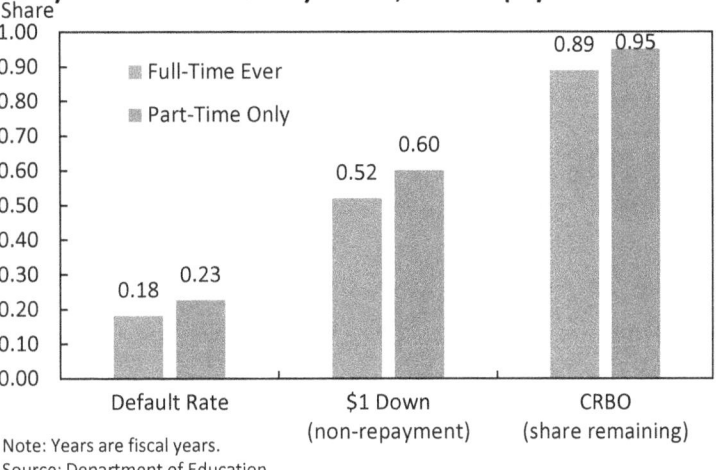

Figure 34. Undergraduate Loan Repayment Outcomes at Year 3 by Enrollment Intensity Status, 2011 Repayment Cohort

Note: Years are fiscal years.
Source: Department of Education

The likelihood of completion is a key driver of differences in repayment outcomes by enrollment intensity. Full-time and part-time borrowers are nearly equally as likely to default after three years if they complete, and the same pattern holds for non-completers. Borrowers who attend part-time only are less than half as likely to complete a degree, however, leading to differences in repayment outcomes by enrollment intensity. The relationship between enrollment intensity and completion underscores the importance of federal student aid policies that lower the number of hours worked while enrolled in college and increase the number of credits taken at a time (Denning 2016).

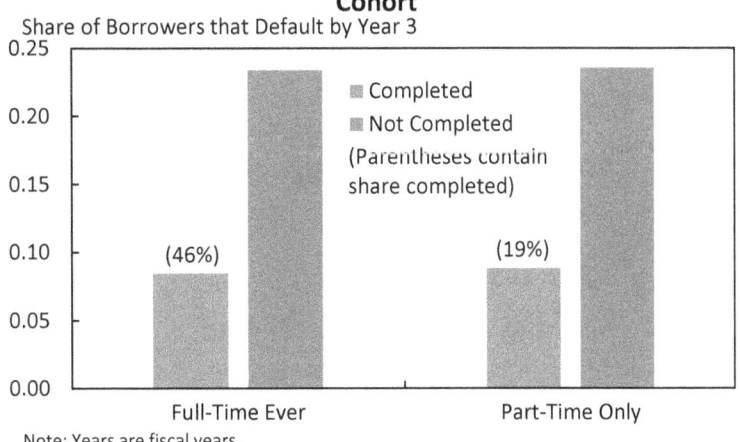

Figure 35. Relationship Between Undergraduate Default and Enrollment Intensity by Completion Status, 2011 Repayment Cohort

Note: Years are fiscal years.
Source: Department of Education

V. Student Loans, Other Individual Outcomes, and the Overall Economy

Federal student loan programs help expand access to high-quality education, which has long-lasting benefits to individuals as well as the overall macroeconomy through higher labor productivity and faster GDP growth. Yet, as noted earlier, some aspects of the recent rise in student loan debt have raised concerns, and there is some concern that the increase in student debt, particularly among individuals attending for-profit institutions, combined with the higher default rates among non-completers, will negatively impact our broader macroeconomy, with some even drawing comparisons to the increase in mortgage debt during the mid-2000s housing bubble. Evidence shows that more indebtedness, regardless of the source of the debt, may limit other economic choices. For example, Dynan (2012) and Mian, Rao, and Sufi (2013) found that individuals with high levels of debt cut their spending more in the Great Recession than those with less debt and that the earlier rise in aggregate debt (primarily mortgages) was large enough that it may have deepened the recession and slowed the recovery.[25]

That individuals with federal student loans can defer repayment or lower their monthly debt payments if their income is initially low is a unique feature that helps limit the negative effects both on the individuals and on the macroeconomy. In addition, individuals with either very small loan balances or with high debt and high income are unlikely to change their other behavior in response to their student debt, again suggesting small impacts on the overall economy from these borrowers. Even among most lower-income borrowers, the increase in their lifetime income from the extra education usually greatly exceeds the debt obligations and should raise other spending over the long term. And yet, for borrowers who did not graduate, attended schools that did not substantially increase their income, or acquired very large debt levels that are not offset by high incomes, the negative side effects of student loans could be substantial.

Comparing the Rise in Student Loans with the Earlier Rise in Mortgage Debt

In terms of the overall economy, the recent rise in student loan debt differs in three important ways from the rise in mortgage debt prior to the Great Recession. These differences, described below, suggest that student loan debt is less likely to make a recession more severe or slow an expansion in the way that mortgage debt may have.

First, despite rising notably over the past decade, student loan debt in aggregate remains low relative to total household disposable income, and student loan debt has risen far less than mortgage debt in the mid-2000s. The nature of student and mortgage debt is different in many ways—most notably, student debt is government guaranteed and has what amounts to payment

---

[25] On the other hand, a rise in the level of debt may not be a general risk factor. Adverse outcomes from leverage such as with the Great Recession likely also depend on the specific reasons for the increase in debt, such as overly optimistic views on house price appreciation or increased credit supply due to securitization. See also Sahm (2014) for a discussion of related research on how household leveraging affects the economy.

renegotiation via PAYE, meaning that the private financial system is not exposed to defaults in the way it was to subprime mortgages.[26] In 2015, total student loan debt was 9 percent of aggregate income, up from 3 percent in 2003, shown in Figure 36.[27] At its peak in 2007, total mortgage debt was 84 percent of aggregate income, up 25 percentage points in less than five years. The subsequent reduction in housing-related leverage in recent years—mortgage debt was back to 61 percent of aggregate income in 2015—has arguably been a headwind to spending growth during the recovery as homeowners paid down debt rather than spending on other items, and in part, this reflects the sheer scale of leverage. Student loan debt may be a meaningful drag on the spending of some borrowers, particularly those who did not complete their degrees; however, the smaller overall scale of student loan debt means that the potential spillovers to the macroeconomy are more limited.

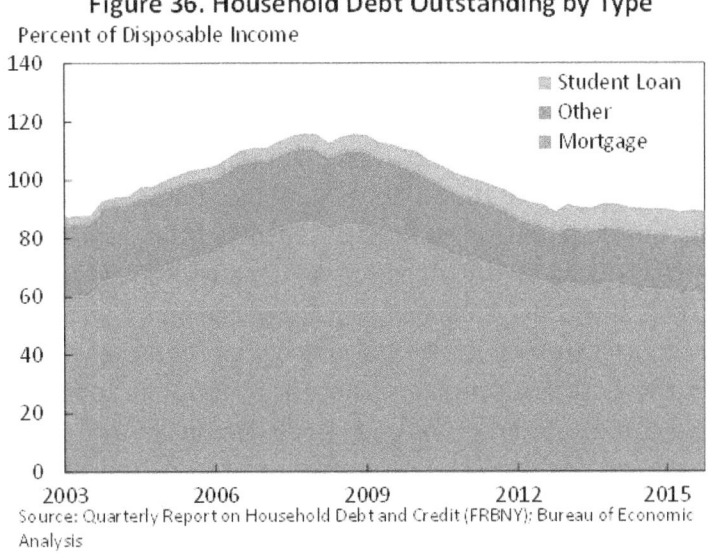

Figure 36. Household Debt Outstanding by Type

Source: Quarterly Report on Household Debt and Credit (FRBNY); Bureau of Economic Analysis

Second, the increase in student loan debt represents a shift in the composition of household debt toward borrowing that can increase future productivity and thus raise overall lifetime income and spending. As Figure 36 shows, the increase in student loan debt has occurred while there was a decrease in other non-student consumer debt, which includes credit cards, home equity

[26] Student loan debt and mortgage debt also differ in many fundamental ways that complicate a comparison. For example, student loans are not backed by collateral, as a mortgage is by a home, and student loans, unlike mortgages, generally cannot be discharged even in bankruptcy. Practices for securitization also differ. While many student loans, along with mortgages, are securitized, federal student loans are explicitly guaranteed by the U.S. government, which limits the private sector losses in the case of default. Finally, access to student loans is less restricted than mortgages (with no credit score or down payment requirements) and there are automatic PAYE programs for student loans to modify repayment plans and defer or reduce monthly payments. Most of the research that find negative macroeconomic effects from debt study mortgage debt, so it is important to think about why those results may not generalize to student loans.

[27] Comparing aggregate debt and aggregate income obscures the fact that student loan debt is a larger portion of debt for younger individuals. Moreover income tends to rise with age, so aggregate debt-to-income ratios are not the same as debt-to-income for individuals. The goal of Figure 36 is to show the overall scale of student loans in the economy.

and auto loans. Unlike borrowing to pay for current spending, student loan debt is an investment in human capital that typically pays off through higher lifetime earnings and increased productivity. College enrollment grew 20 percent between 2005 and 2010—a larger increase than any five-year period since the 1970s. Historical experience has shown that a more educated workforce is a key factor in productivity growth (Aaronson and Sullivan 2001). Of course, this positive effect depends on the quality of the additional education and not simply the quantity. The main macroeconomic impact of student loans, particularly over the longer run, is via the boost to output and productivity from a more educated workforce. To the extent that an increase in student loan balances represents the same level of education but at higher cost to the student, the downsides may be present with no new education, but the rise in educational attainment suggests at least some of this debt was funding an increase in educational levels.

Third, the indirect costs of higher education, in terms of foregone earnings, fell during the Great Recession, which played a role in raising enrollment and student debt. From the perspective of economic theory, the marked step up in college attendance and borrowing during the Great Recession was an efficient response to the economic conditions. The unemployment rate roughly doubled from 2007 to 2009, substantially lowering the implicit cost of college in terms of the foregone earnings while attending. At that time, getting more education was the best option for more individuals, since the demand for workers, especially lower-skilled and less-experienced workers, was temporarily reduced by the recession. Yet, many of the resources often used to pay for higher education, such as income and savings from parents and students and private-sector credit, also decreased during the recession. The uninterrupted access to government student loans, as reinforced in the Ensuring Continued Access to Student Loans Act of 2010, and the expansion of federal grants in the Student Aid and Fiscal Responsibility Act of 2009 and tax credits for education in the American Recovery and Reinvestment Act of 2009, allowed more individuals to use the recession—a time of low current earnings—to invest in their future earnings potential.

While it is still important to monitor in overall leverage, on net, student loan debt is still likely to be a boost to the economy over the longer run by increasing educational levels and workers' skills.

Student Loans and Homeownership

Despite the positive long-run impacts, in the near term as the labor market was still recovering from the Great Recession, higher student loan debt may have weighed on some areas of the economy. A college education can raise earnings net of student debt interest payments and result in more home ownership. But for a given amount of college education, additional debt can reduce homeownership among young adults (Brown et al. 2014; Mezza et al. 2016). But, based on two sets of studies, the rise in student debt has only played a small role in the fact that the homeownership rate among individuals aged 24 to 32 fell from 42 percent in 2005 to 33 percent in 2014.

Higher education, even paid for by debt, raises the likelihood of owning a home because of its impact on future earnings. Figure 37 shows that in the fourth quarter of 2005, 9 percent of individuals aged 25 to 30 with current (non-delinquent) student loan debt purchased a home by taking out a new mortgage.[28] This exceeded the 6 percent for individuals without student loan debt (which includes both those who did not attend college and those who did attend college but did not borrow). Those with student loan debts above $50,000 were actually more likely (11 percent) than all student loan borrowers to buy a home. Yet, this relationship in the cross section between student loan debt and buying a home does not necessarily capture the causal effect of higher debt on homeownership. In particular, individuals who pursue graduate or professional degrees tend to have higher future earnings, an outcome that both supports more student loan borrowing as well as more homeownership. Still, many of the individuals in this analysis without student loans did not attend college, which would imply lower earnings and fewer resources to buy a home.[29]

Individuals who have student loans but are delinquent on repaying those loans are the least likely to buy a home. Many of these defaults are on very small loan balances, as discussed earlier, so the student loans are probably not the main obstacle to buying a home. The lack of home buying among those in default on small student loan balances is more likely due to their limited economic resources, in general. Low levels of income or assets would both leave them unable to make student loan payments as well as take on any large purchase. Still, defaulting on student loans may also limit their ability to buy a home.

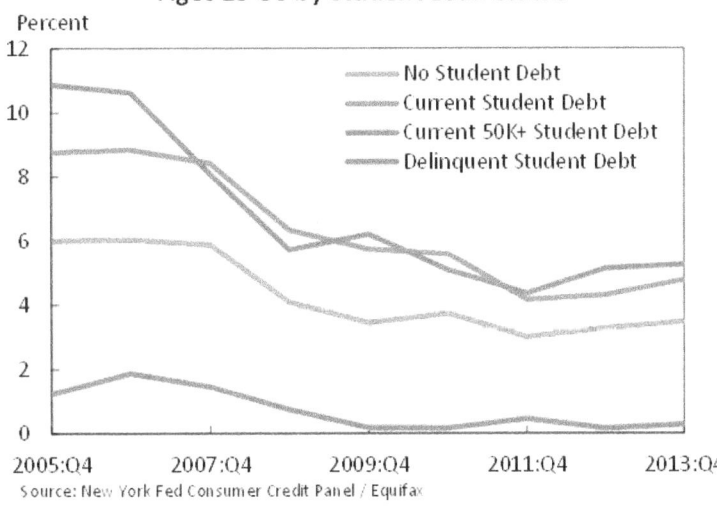

Figure 37. Rate of New Mortgage Originations, Ages 25-30 by Student Loan Status

Source: New York Fed Consumer Credit Panel / Equifax

Looking, instead, at the changes over time in home buying, there is some evidence that student loan debt may increasingly have been an impediment to home buying. (See also Brown et al

---

[28] These data are from the FRBNY Consumer Credit Panel / Equifax, a sample of individual credit records, which has detailed financial information but little demographic information on the borrowers. The information on the level of student loan debt and mortgage debt is high quality but there is no information on education attainment, type of institution attended, or the loan characteristics, including whether it is a federal or private loan.

[29] See Bricker et al. (2015) for a discussion of the available data on student loans with a comparison of estimates from credit records and household surveys.

2014.) The rate of home buying has fallen for all the groups in Figure 37; however, the decline was larger for individuals with student loan debt.

Changes in the composition of student loan borrowers in the last decade, as discussed earlier in the report, complicate the interpretation of the time series trends in Figure 37. The median earnings of student loan borrowers two years after they entered repayment in 2005 and 2012 declined from $36,250 to $29,500 (in 2014 dollars) (Looney and Yannelis 2015), which would have lowered the likelihood of buying a home. In part, this decline in median earnings reflects the negative effect of the severe recession and the ongoing labor market recovery on wages and unemployment—challenges that affected both borrowers and non-borrowers. In addition, it reflects an increase in the share of student loan borrowers attending community colleges or for-profit schools, who have lower earnings potential and thus a lower likelihood of home buying. Thus many of the additional student loan borrowers in recent years have come from groups that, even without student loans (and the education it paid for), would have been less likely to buy a home than the student loan borrowers in the past.

Work by Mezza, Sommer, and Sherlund (2014) shows that while early in life those with college education and no debt are more likely to be homeowners than those without debt, by age 34, the homeownership rates are nearly identical (Figure 38). And the homeownership rate of college attendees by age 34, regardless of whether they have student debt or not, is more than 10 percentage points higher than of those without a college education. It is education, not student debt, that drives the persistent differences in homeownership.

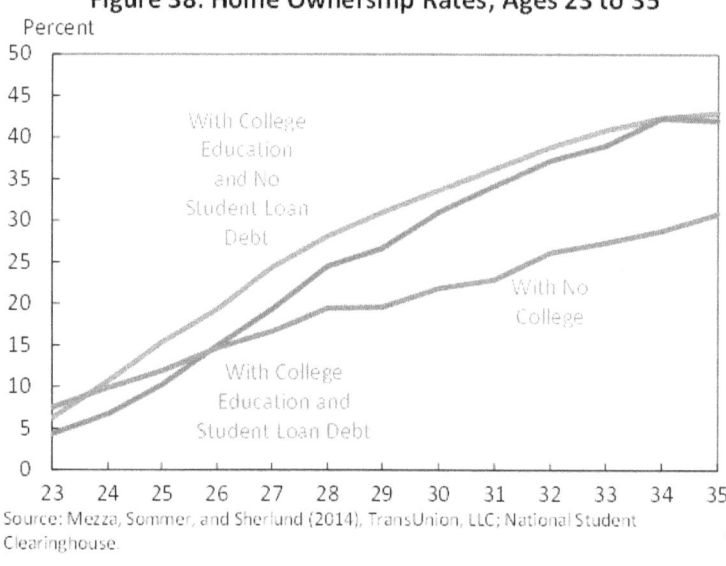

Figure 38. Home Ownership Rates, Ages 23 to 35

Source: Mezza, Sommer, and Sherlund (2014), TransUnion, LLC; National Student Clearinghouse.

But for a given amount of education, taking on more debt can result in somewhat less homeownership, as shown in Figure 38 and verified by more careful research that takes into account the observable characteristics of student borrowers, such as the type of degree. For example, Cooper and Wang (2014) estimate that a 10 percent increase in student loan debt for a borrower is associated with a half a percentage point lower likelihood of homeownership.

Moreover, the authors estimate this association by holding constant the differences in demographics, family income, degree characteristics, occupation and industry, and location across individuals with some college experience. A separate analysis by Houle and Berger (2015) using a different data set finds a similar result.[30]

Work by Mezza et al. (2016) tries to identify the causal relationship and finds a larger, negative estimate of student debt on homeownership.[31] Using only the variation in student loan debt due to differences in home-state tuition, they estimate that a 10 percent increase in student loan debt leads to a 1 to 2 percentage point decline in homeownership rates for the borrower. Their estimated effect of student loan debt on homeownership is larger than the Cooper and Wang (2014) or Houle and Berger (2015) studies. It is important to note that all of these studies focus on younger households, so it is possible that rising student loans have delayed but not reduced lifetime homeownership. In addition, these studies hold constant the level of education such that they focus only on the impact of debt, not on the education that the debt helped to fund, thereby excluding the positive boost to homeownership from increased education-related earnings.

The homeownership rate for those ages 24 to 32 fell by 9 percentage points from 2005 to 2014. Over the same period the average student loan debt rose 42 percent. Using the estimates from Cooper and Wang, this increase in student loan debt lowered the average homeownership rate of individuals with student debt by 2.1 percentage points. In contrast, the much larger estimates from Mezza et al., suggest a decline of 6.3 percentage points. However, only 30 percent of young households had student loan debt in 2005, so the estimated decline in overall homeownership for all young households due to rising student loan debt is 0.6 to 1.9 percentage points.[32] Figure 39 shows this graphically. As noted above, homeownership among young households fell by 9.0 percentage points between 2005 and 2014 (the blue bar). Had there been no increase in average student debt over this period, the homeownership rate of all young households would either have fallen by 8.4 percent (the red bar), based on Cooper and Wang, or by 7.1 percentage points (the green bar), using Mezza et al. The back-of-the-envelope summary of existing research in Figure 39 shows relatively modest homeownership effects from the increase in the level of student loan debt. These estimates focus on the impact of a larger average loan balance, essentially asking if the same borrower received fewer grants and more loans (or tuition increased), what is the impact on their home buying. The analysis in Figure 39 does not consider whether there is an impact from there being more borrowers (a negative), more defaults (a negative) which are discussed below, or the fact that due to the loans there are more people with education (a positive). Many other factors have affected homeownership among young households including preferences, the state of the macroeconomy and job markets, and tighter conditions for mortgage lending. The small homeownership effects suggest small overall macroeconomic impacts.

---

[30] Cooper and Wang (2014) use 1988 National Educational Longitudinal Survey (NELS88). Houle and Berger (2015) use the National Longitudinal Study of Youth 1997 cohort.

[31] Mezza et al. (2016) use an administrative panel data set. Their sample includes individuals who were aged 23 to 31 in 2004 and they have data on these individuals from 1997 to 2010.

[32] According to the data set constructed by Mezza et al. (2016), 60 percent of individuals aged 23-31 in 2003 attended college and, of those who attended, only 52 percent took out student loans.

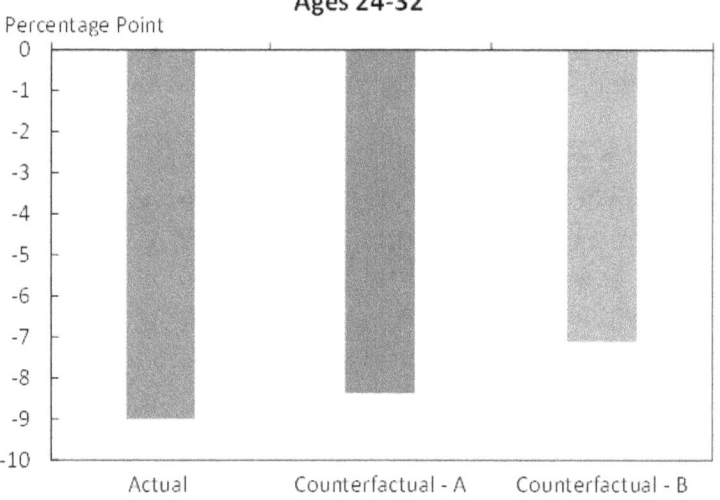

Figure 39. Change in Homeownership Rate 2005 to 2014, Ages 24-32

Young individuals have clearly reduced their home buying since the mid-2000s. The modest role of student loan debt in the decline in home ownership by young households is underscored by the fact that homeownership rates have also fallen steeply for those who did not attend college. This suggests that other factors beyond student loan debt must be affecting home ownership. Figure 40 shows that the decline is not particularly different for those who attended college and those who did not. Lower wages, reduced private sector credit, and a challenging job market for new entrants are more likely the primary drivers of this decline.

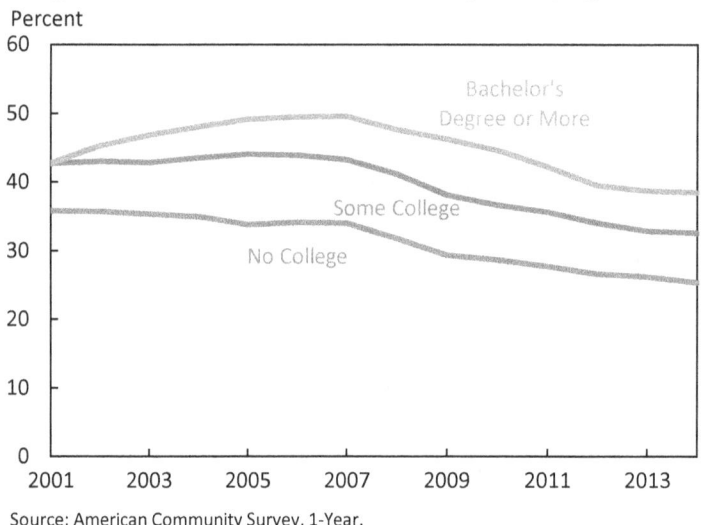

Figure 40. Household Homeownership Rates, Ages 24-32

Source: American Community Survey, 1-Year.

Young households are only a portion of the overall population and a portion of those with student loan debt, so changes in their home buying behavior are only a partial window to changes in the overall housing market related to student loan debt. Still, homeownership rates have fallen noticeably across households of all ages and education levels, suggesting student loan debt is only one factor in the housing market.[33] Note that the limited macroeconomic effects we find from rising student loan debt do not diminish the effects on individuals, and even if rising student loan balances were not a primary driver of the decline in homeownership, deferred repayment options, such as with PAYE, can help make homeownership more feasible.

Beyond the impact of higher average balances, the increase in the number of individuals with high levels of student debt, as shown in Looney and Yannelis (2015), may have an additional effect on economic outcomes. The percent of borrowers with student loan balances over $50,000 (in 2013 dollars) rose from 5.1 percent in 2000 to 13.7 percent in 2014. As noted earlier, high-debt individuals are actually more likely to own a home than lower-debt individuals, largely due to their higher earnings potential. Yet, the composition of high-debt borrowers has also shifted somewhat away from those with graduate education (80 percent of high-debtors in 2000 to 62 percent in 2014). The rising share of undergraduates among high-debt students was particularly pronounced for those attending for-profit schools (2 percent of high-debtors in 2000 to 11 percent in 2014). High student debt without high earnings potential is a real hardship for individuals and an important policy concern, but the macroeconomic impacts are limited by the relatively small numbers. About 2 percent of all households in 2014 had high student debt and less than a half percent had high debt and only undergraduate education, though these ratios are higher among young households. Policies that provide better information to prospective students may help avoid mismatching debt and future earnings.

While the increase in the level of student loan debt appears to have had at most small negative macroeconomic effects, rising default and delinquency rates are a concern. Defaulting on student loan debt is a sign of acute financial distress and makes it more costly to borrow for other large purchases, such as a home or a car, due to a lower credit score. The three-year default rate on federal loans was 6 percentage points higher for those who began repayment in 2012 than in 2004.[34] The rise in default rates led to 1.3 million more defaults within the first three years of repayment among those who began repaying in 2008 to 2012. Still, even if all these additional defaulters would have otherwise bought a home (which is unlikely), they can account for at most a percentage point lower home ownership rate (among all ages) in 2015. In fact, the effect of rising student loan defaults on homeownership is likely much smaller since not all of these individuals would have bought homes. For example, roughly one third of the defaulters had less than $5,000 in student loan debt. It seems unlikely that these borrowers would have bought a house in the absence of student debt as they are likely constrained by low income. Moreover, Mezza and Sommer (2015) found individuals who later defaulted on student loan debt had lower

---

[33] See also Devlin-Foltz and Sabelhaus (forthcoming) for empirical evidence that broad-based shocks to income and wealth have been the primary drivers of changes in economic behavior before, during and after the Great Recession. And yet, reduced demand for starter homes by young adults may be having indirect effects on the overall housing market, as discussed by Ortalo-Magne and Rady (2006).

[34] The 3-year cohort default rate from the Department of Education is the percentage of a borrowers who enter repayment on certain federal loans during a federal fiscal year (October 1 to September 30) and default prior to the end of the next one to two fiscal years. This metric provides a somewhat narrow view of defaults since it is limited to federal student loans and does not examine defaults after the third year. For example, using credit records with all types of student loans, Brown et al. (2015) show that default rates continue to rise after the third year.

credit scores prior to leaving school, suggesting that these individuals would have faced hurdles to homeownership even without student debt. Nevertheless, as Figure 37 shows, those who are delinquent on any student loans (federal or private) have very low rates of home buying. Student loans may not be the cause of their financial distress but it is a negative outcome for those individuals and worth avoiding. In fact, the Administration has supported income-based repayment and Gainful Employment regulations as ways to help lower defaults.

Student Loans and Other Economic Outcomes

The housing market is, of course, only one area in which the rise in student loan debt could be having macroeconomic impacts. Research looking at other behaviors, such as car buying or entrepreneurship, faces similar challenges as home buying in identifying the causal effects of student loans. In terms of consumer spending, Brown and Caldwell (2013) show the fraction of 25-year olds with auto loan debt has fallen more sharply since the recession for individuals with student loan debt than those without. This suggests that the rise in student loan debt may be weighing on debt-financed auto purchases. Yet, Kurz and Li (2015) find that, in general, individuals with higher student loan balances are somewhat more likely to buy a car, though those with very high levels of debt (in the 90th percentile of balances) are substantially less likely to make car purchases. With the negative impact of student loans on auto buying concentrated in a small portion of individuals, the impact on the overall auto market is limited and, given the record auto sales in 2015, may have dissipated.

In terms of entrepreneurship, Ambrose, Cordell, and Ma (2015) find that counties in which student loan debt rose more relative to other kinds of debt from 2000 to 2010 also experienced slower growth in the number of small businesses (firms with 1-4 employees). Using different data and an approach to estimate causal effects, Krishan and Wang (2015) find that an increase in student loan balances lowered the likelihood of owning a small business as well as the average level of business income. These results may be related to the fact that student loan debt cannot be discharged in bankruptcy and thus makes individuals with student loan debt less able to take on the risks of owning a business. The macroeconomic impact of lower entrepreneurship is hard to quantify, but the slowdown in the business startup rate began at least in the 1970s and is largely or entirely driven by other factors (Decker et al. 2014).

On net, student debt is a burden to some households, but the increase in student debt does not appear to have substantially altered the macroeconomic conditions. Had the same students received an education without as many loans, the recovery would likely have been stronger, but not substantially so. Most individuals, and the economy as a whole, will benefit from the education made possible by student loans. Nonetheless, the rise in defaults and high debt among low earners show that student loans can have negative effects on some individuals and merit a policy response.

VI.   Administration Efforts to Help Students Better Invest

Over the last seven years, the Obama Administration has taken great strides to help students make more effective investments in higher education. These efforts have been targeted to address the market failures and procedural complexities identified in Section I by helping to offset the cost of college, incentivizing higher completion rates, providing better information about the costs and benefits of colleges, holding the most poorly performing colleges accountable, simplifying the financial aid application process, and expanding access to flexible repayment plans that help ease credit constraints. Despite these important steps, more work remains to ensure that all students are able to pursue higher education if they desire and that they can do so affordably.

Helping to Offset College Costs

One way the Administration has helped to reduce credit constraints and ensure the social benefits of higher education are realized is by directly offsetting the cost of college for many students, especially those from low-income families. Economics research confirms the positive impact of lowering college costs, showing that it increases the probability of college attendance and helps students complete. For example, Dynarski (2003) examines the elimination of the Social Security Student Benefit Program in 1982, and her estimates suggest that an offer of $1,000 in grant aid increases the probability of attending college by about 3.6 percentage points and appears to increase completed schooling. Abraham and Clark (2006) find similar impacts on college attendance in their study of the District of Columbia Tuition Assistance Grant Program instituted in 1999. More recent research specific to community colleges shows that for high school graduates, a $1,000 decrease in community college tuition increased immediate enrollment by 7.1 percentage points (Denning 2016).

Under the Obama Administration, supports to students to lower college costs have increased in meaningful ways, including increases in Pell Grant funding. Since coming into office, President Obama has worked aggressively to increase the maximum Pell award because Pell Grants are the primary form of financial aid for many students to pay tuition. Today, on average, Pell Grants reduce the cost of college by $3,700 for 8 million students a year. Pell Grant funding increased by more than $12 billion from academic year 2008-2009 to 2014-2015, a 67 percent increase, and the maximum Pell Grant award has increased by $1,000. Moreover, for the first time, Pell Grant funding has been tied to inflation to ensure the value of the aid does not fall over time, and the President's 2017 budget proposes to index Pell in 2017 and beyond.

The Administration has also reduced the cost of college for low- and middle-income families through tax credits. In 2009, the Administration established the American Opportunity Tax Credit (AOTC), which provides a maximum credit of $2,500 per year—or up to $10,000 over four years— to expand and replace the Hope higher education credit. Along with supporting a wider range of families, the AOTC also better targets low-income families. Before the AOTC, only 5 percent of credit and tuition deduction dollars went to filers with incomes under $25,000; in 2012, that share rose to 24 percent (Dynarski and Scott-Clayton 2016). The AOTC will cut taxes by over

$1,800 on average for nearly 10 million families in 2016, and the bipartisan tax and budget agreement that President Obama signed into law in December 2015 made the AOTC permanent.

Finally, the proposal for America's College Promise, which would make two years of community college free for responsible students, would also help expand college access. While student loans can serve as an effective tool to allow individuals to invest in their educations, for many students, especially disadvantaged students, this is not enough. President Obama has stated that all responsible students should be able to attend college, and the Administration has put forward a proposal to make two years of community college as free and universal as high school. Free community college not only reduces the credit constraints faced by low-income students, it also eliminates the information barriers related to the cost and complexities of applying for aid. Removing these barriers at community colleges is especially important, as community college students tend to be poorer than students attending four-year schools—over half of community college students have family incomes below 185 percent of the federal poverty line—and are less likely to have parents who attended college to help them navigate the student aid application process (NPSAS 2012, CEA tabulations). If all states participate, an estimated 9 million students could benefit, and a full-time community college student could save an average of $3,800 in tuition per year. Evaluations of early local Promise programs, such as Kalamazoo Promise and Knox Achieves, show that these programs can improve high school graduation, college enrollment, and college graduation rates (Bartik and Lachowska 2013; Bartik, Hershbein, and Lachowska 2015; Carruthers and Fox 2016).

Incentivizing Completion

To further decrease costs and increase completion rates, the Administration has encouraged greater innovation and a stronger evidence base around effective strategies to promote college access and success through 42 First in the World (FITW) grants that support the implementation and evaluation of innovative and evidence-based interventions at institutions across the nation. This program targets adult learners, working students, part-time students, students from low-income backgrounds, students of color, students with disabilities, first-generation students, and other students at risk for not persisting in or completing college. In addition, through the Experimental Sites Initiative, the Administration has piloted reforms to existing higher education policies.

Additionally, the Administration included two Pell proposals in its 2017 Budget to promote completion among low-income students. First, the Pell for Accelerated Completion program would make Pell Grant funds available year-round to students who are taking a full course load and who have exhausted their awards; and second, the On-Track Pell Bonus would increase students' Pell Grants by $300 each year if they take at least 15 credit hours per semester, the amount typically needed to complete a two- or four-year degree on-time. The incentives created by these policies are supported by research showing that performance-based aid improves persistence and completion (MDRC 2016). Another proposal focused on promoting completion, the College Opportunity and Graduation Bonus, would provide institutional grants to colleges that enroll and graduate many low-income students on time and provide an incentive for these institutions to improve their completion rates for low-income students.

Improving Information

Research shows that when students have better information, they make better choices about their education. When choosing a college, students need information on college quality and cost to know whether their investment in higher education will pay off. For high-achieving, low-income students, research shows that providing information that compares details about college cost and quality, like semi-customized net price and graduation rates, enables students to attend and progress at schools that better match their qualifications (Hoxby and Turner 2013). Further research shows that clear and detailed information about earnings can lead students to revise their employment expectations and change their major choice (Ruder and Van Noy 2014). Accessible information about costs and economic outcomes thus plays a crucial role in encouraging students to make informed decisions about enrolling in higher education and choosing the best college for their needs.

The Administration has recognized the importance of information in encouraging students to attend a quality college. In 2015, the Department of Education launched the redesigned College Scorecard to help empower Americans to select colleges based on what matters most to them. Importantly, the Scorecard provides information on how well institutions are serving students of all backgrounds, and it highlights institutions that focus on placing a quality, affordable education within reach. Students and the public can now access the most reliable, comprehensive, and nationally comparable data on outcomes at specific colleges, including former students' earnings, student debt by completion status, and borrowers' repayment rates. The Scorecard provides this information for about 4,500 colleges and includes detailed breakdowns by demographic group, allowing all students to assess how well these colleges are serving students like themselves before deciding where to apply and attend. To date, over 1.3 million visitors have accessed the new College Scorecard. The Administration has also partnered with outside organizations and made the data freely available to researchers and developers to help expand the reach of Scorecard information. Preliminary research provides some suggestive evidence that the College Scorecard has helped students decide where to send their college applications (Hurwitz and Smith 2016).

In 2015, the Administration also announced an earlier and easier process for applying for federal financial aid, allowing students to apply to colleges and for financial aid in tandem. Beginning in 2016, FAFSA applicants will be able to complete the form on October 1st for the following academic year. Students and their families will now get a reliable understanding of their aid eligibility as early as the fall—the same time that many high school students are searching for, applying to, and even selecting colleges. An earlier FAFSA helps clear an important hurdle in reducing information barriers related to cost, and the Administration is working with states and colleges to provide financial aid award information on this earlier timeline as well.

In addition, the Department's Gainful Employment regulation requires career college programs to provide key information on costs, whether students graduate, how much they earn, and how much debt they may accumulate. Regulations from 2010 also strengthen the Department's authority to take action against institutions engaging in deceptive advertising, marketing, and sales practices. These regulations will help prevent students from choosing poor quality colleges and taking on unmanageable debt.

The Obama Administration is also proposing new protections for borrowers and taxpayers against fraud, deception, and other misconduct by postsecondary institutions. One provision of the proposed regulation would require proprietary institutions to warn prospective and enrolled students, individually and through promotional materials, if their students have very poor loan repayment outcomes. The proposed regulations also would establish a number of triggers and early-warning events, many of which would automatically require schools to put up funds, in the form of letters of credit (LOCs), that total at least 10 percent of the amount of Title IV funds received by the school over the previous year. Institutions that set off the triggers would be required to warn their prospective and enrolled students that they have been required to provide this financial protection to the Department.

Protecting Students from Low-Quality Schools

Although improved information helps students select better colleges, more direct action is sometimes needed. With the Gainful Employment regulations, the Administration will cut off federal aid to career college programs that consistently fail accountability standards. While many career college programs are helping to prepare America's workforce for the jobs of the future, far too many students at these schools are taking on unsustainable debt in exchange for degrees and certificates that fail to help them get the jobs they need or were promised.

Under the Gainful Employment regulation, programs whose graduates have annual loan payments less than 8 percent of total earnings or less than 20 percent of discretionary earnings are considered to have passed the requirements. Programs whose graduates have annual loan payments between 8 percent and 12 percent of total earnings or between 20 percent and 30 percent of discretionary earnings are considered to be "in the warning zone" and at risk of failing the requirements. Programs are deemed to have failed the requirements if their graduates have annual loan payments greater than 12 percent of total earnings and greater than 30 percent of discretionary earnings. Programs that fail in two out of any three consecutive years or are in the zone for four consecutive years are no longer eligible for federal student aid for a minimum of three years.

Based on available data, the Department of Education estimates that about 1,400 programs serving 840,000 students—of which 99 percent are at for-profit institutions—would not pass the accountability standards. All programs will have the opportunity to make immediate changes that could help them avoid sanctions, but if these programs do not improve, they will ultimately become ineligible for federal student aid—which often makes up nearly 90 percent of the revenue at for-profit institutions.

The Obama Administration is proposing new protections for borrowers and taxpayers against fraud, deception, and other misconduct by postsecondary institutions. The proposed regulations would create a clear, consistent, and transparent process for borrowers who have been harmed by their school's misconduct to seek debt relief, along with new warnings to help students steer clear of poorly performing proprietary schools. The proposed regulations would also protect taxpayers by requiring schools to provide greater financial protection to the Federal government based upon early indicators of school financial distress. In addition, the proposed regulations include measures that would end the use of both so-called "pre-dispute, mandatory arbitration agreements" and of class action bans that prevent students from having their day in court.

These regulations build upon a record of action by this Administration which has encouraged states to step up oversight in their role as authorizers, encouraged accreditors to focus on student outcomes, and created a new student aid enforcement unit to respond more quickly and efficiently to allegations of illegal actions by higher education institutions.

Simplifying Aid

As described in Section I, the complexity of the FAFSA has created barriers to efficiency and equity in the distribution of student financial aid, deterring many students who would benefit from aid from applying. It follows that reducing this complexity should help students access federal student aid to better invest in their education, and the research supports this conclusion. In particular, the evidence shows that providing assistance with filling out the FAFSA encourages students to apply for aid and enroll in college. In an experiment where tax professionals assisted families in filling out their FAFSA and provided personalized aid estimates, students were significantly more likely to file the FAFSA and enroll in college; the college enrollment impact was even greater for students from low-income families (Bettinger et al. 2012).

In light of the evidence about the benefits of simplifying aid, the Administration has undertaken a number of reforms to streamline the FAFSA process. The Administration has revamped the online form for all families so they can skip questions that are not relevant to them. In addition, over 6 million students and parents took advantage of the ability to electronically retrieve their income information from the IRS when completing their 2014-2015 FAFSA, an innovation that improves both speed and accuracy. During the 2014-2015 application cycle, students and families on average filled out the FAFSA in about 20 minutes, only one third of the time it took seven years ago.

In past years a significant portion of FAFSA filers have been unable to electronically retrieve their income and tax information from the IRS because they had not yet filed their tax returns before completing their FAFSA forms. For example, 34 percent of parents of dependent students had not yet filed their 2013 tax returns when they were completing their 2014-2015 FAFSA. Such applicants had to manually input their estimated income and tax information into their FAFSA, or worse did not submit a timely FAFSA because they erroneously believed that they were not allowed to do so unless then had filed their tax returns. Among other advantages of moving the FAFSA process earlier (beginning October 1) and using prior-prior year income is that the relationship between FAFSA filing and tax return filing becomes moot. Thus, we expect to see an increase in the number of students and parents who use the IRS Data Retrieval Tool. This will not only simplify the aid application process for students and their families and reduce the burden on institutions, it will also improve the accuracy of the information used in the determination of students' aid eligibility.

In addition, President Obama has called upon Congress to further simplify the FAFSA by removing questions regarding savings, investments, and net worth, and eliminating questions related to untaxed income and exclusions from income that are not reported to the IRS. In all, up to 30 burdensome and unnecessarily complex questions would be eliminated, shortening the FAFSA application substantially, and making it easier for students and families to access critical resources to pay for college.

Providing More Flexible Repayment Plans

As described in Section I, the constraint imposed for many borrowers by the traditional standard, 10-year student loan repayment plan (that students are enrolled in by default) can hinder debt management since it requires the same monthly payment at the beginning of a borrower's career, when earnings are lowest, as it does mid-career. This can dissuade students from investing in their education even when the investment has large net benefits over a lifetime. The Administration has made payment plans more flexible and loan payments more manageable through the expansion of income-driven repayment plans. Income driven repayment plans increase flexibility in several ways. First, by expanding the period of repayment, individuals can spread their student loan payments over a longer period of time, while retaining the option of paying sooner with no pre-payment penalty. Second, by tying payments to borrowers' incomes, income driven repayment plans link the timing of repayment more closely with the time path of earnings gains from higher education, and they remove needless credit constraints in times when income is temporarily low. Finally, income driven repayment plans can serve as a form of insurance against uncertainty, helping to address some barriers associated with risk.

With the new expansions, borrowers will never have to pay more than 10 percent of their discretionary income to repay their debt. The Administration initially expanded income-driven repayment with the Pay-As-You-Earn (PAYE) plan in 2012, which reduced monthly payments to 10 percent of borrowers' discretionary income, lower than the 15 percent required under the original Income Based Repayment Plan in place. Under PAYE, students could also have their remaining loan balances forgiven after 20 years of qualifying payments, 5 years earlier than the original Income Based Repayment plan. PAYE extended more affordable loans to 1.6 million borrowers; however, many borrowers remained ineligible. That is why in 2015, the Administration expanded PAYE with the Revised-Pay-As-You-Earn (REPAYE) repayment plan which expanded eligibility to all Direct Loan student borrowers, including any student with a Direct Loan or a consolidated loan (excluding PLUS loans to parents).

Figure 41 below illustrates how the theoretical repayment curve for the standard 10-year plan differs from REPAYE for a typical borrower graduating with a four-year degree.[35] Data from the Baccalaureate and Beyond study show that seniors graduating college in 2008 held a median debt of $17,125 and earned a median income of $31,000 upon leaving school. The figure assumes an interest rate of 4.29 percent consistent with the current student loan rate, real earnings growth consistent with trends in Figure 6, 2 percent inflation, and a single-person family (for ease of REPAYE calculations). The Standard line corresponds to the standard 10-year repayment plan with an initial income of $31,000 and an initial debt of $17,125, consistent with the Baccalaureate and Beyond data. REPAYE 1 uses the REPAYE formula with the same initial income and debt, while REPAYE 2 uses the same initial income but an initial debt of $31,000 to show how repayment patterns differ by debt amounts. The Standard plan line is relatively flat, reflecting the constant rate at which the principal balance is paid off under this plan. In contrast, both the REPAYE lines show that principal repayment is initially slow and accelerates over time. Further, a comparison of the two REPAYE lines shows that the larger the debt is in comparison to income (or the smaller income is in comparison to debt), the less the REPAYE repayment curve will look like the Standard curve.

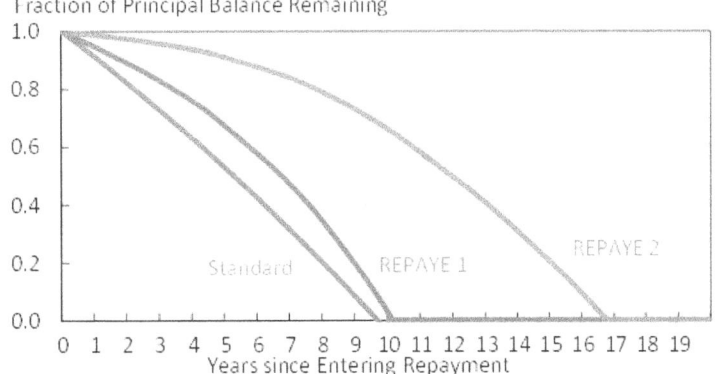

Figure 41. Repayment Distribution by Repayment Plan

Note: Calculations assume a real interest rate of 3.76%, 2% inflation, income growth corresponding with Figure xx describing earnings by age for full-time full-year workers, that borrowers are in single-person families, and assumptions about income and debt from the 2008 Baccalaureate and Beyond Study. REPAYE 1 and 2 differ in their original principal debt amounts.
Source: CEA Calculations

Continuing to expand enrollment in income driven repayment plans for students who would benefit remains a key priority for this Administration. As of the first quarter of fiscal year 2016, about 4.8 million (roughly 1 in 5) borrowers with federally managed debt were enrolled in income driven repayment plans. The share of borrowers with federally managed debt enrolled in income driven repayment has quadrupled over the last four years from 5 percent in the first quarter of fiscal year 2012 to 20 percent in the first quarter of fiscal year 2016. To achieve this increase, the Administration has used tools such as behavioral "nudges," improved loan servicer contract requirements, efforts associated with the President's Student Aid Bill of Rights, a student debt

---

[35] It should be noted that a number of alternative repayment plans also exist, some of which have longer payment schedules.

challenge to gather commitments from external stakeholders, and increased and improved targeted outreach to key borrower segments who would benefit from PAYE. Although barriers related to recertifying income and interfacing with the income driven repayment enrollment tools online persist, the Administration is exploring options for how to address these remaining shortcomings.

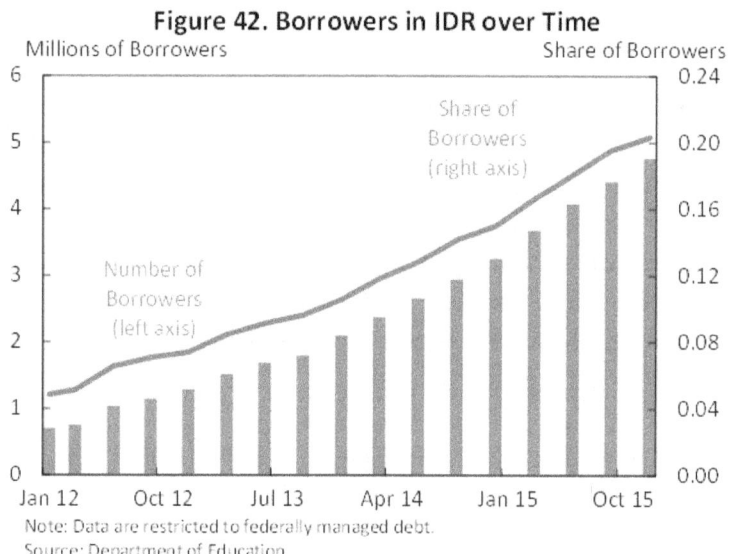

Figure 42. Borrowers in IDR over Time

Note: Data are restricted to federally managed debt.
Source: Department of Education

New Department of Education data offer insights about the types of borrowers that have enrolled in income driven repayment. In general, the data show that income driven repayment borrowers tend to have lower reported family incomes than borrowers on the standard repayment plan. Among borrowers with undergraduate loans enrolled in income driven repayment as of the third quarter of fiscal year 2015, the average family income (in real 2014 dollars) based on the first FAFSA filed was $45,000, compared to $57,000 for those on the standard repayment plan. For borrowers with graduate loans, the average income among those enrolled in income driven repayment was $60,000, compared to $74,000 for borrowers on the standard repayment plan. Even within sectors of educational institutions, borrowers enrolled in income driven repayment tend to come from lower income backgrounds than borrowers in the standard repayment plan. One factor contributing to lower incomes among undergraduate income driven repayment enrollees is that these borrowers are more likely to be classified as independent, and independent borrowers tended to have lower reported incomes since their parents' incomes are not counted as part of their family's income. Overall, 52 percent of borrowers in income driven repayment were classified as independent, as opposed to 42 percent of borrowers under the standard repayment plan.

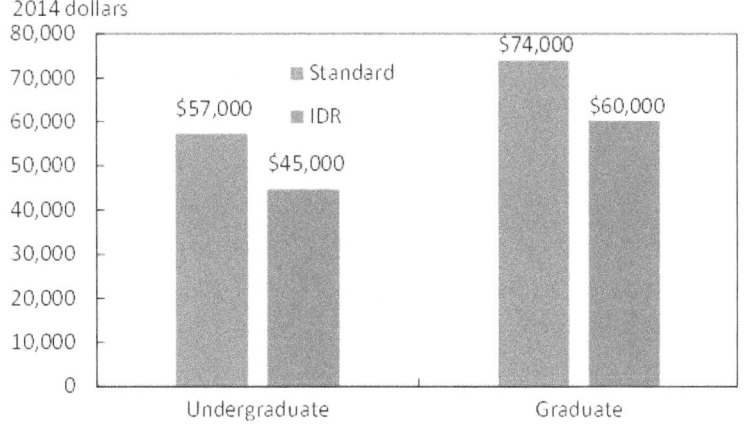

Figure 43. Average Family Income by Repayment Plan

Note: Data are as of the third quarter of fiscal year 2015. Income based on first FAFSA filed, converted to 2014 dollars. Undergraduate and graduate are broken apart at the loan level.
Source: Department of Education

Given that income driven repayment plans tend to change repayment schedules more dramatically for borrowers whose debt is high relative to their income, it is perhaps unsurprising that income driven repayment enrollees tend to have graduate loans and to have larger debt volumes outstanding. For example, 30 percent of income driven repayment borrowers have graduate loans, compared to 10 percent of borrowers under the standard repayment plan. Relatedly, borrowers in income driven repayment tend to have larger loan balances outstanding than borrowers on the standard plan, with a median debt amount of $34,000 compared to $10,000. Although this difference partly reflects the larger share of graduate borrowers enrolled in income driven repayment, differences remain even among graduate and undergraduate borrowers. Undergraduate-only borrowers in income driven repayment have a median outstanding debt of $25,000 compared with $10,000 in the standard plan. The disparity is even wider among graduate borrowers, who typically owe $86,000 for those in income driven repayment, compared to $23,000 for those under the standard plan. These differences in outstanding balances also remain when looking within sector, and they are in part driven by the fact that borrowers entering income driven repayment typically have larger principal loan balances than borrowers in the standard repayment plan (according to data for the 2011 repayment cohort).

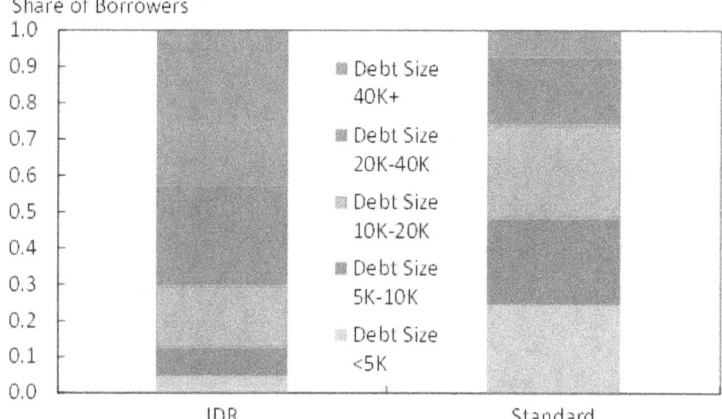

Figure 44. Size of Outstanding Loan Balance by Repayment Plan

Share of Borrowers

Note: Data are as of the third quarter of fiscal year 2015. Debt size is based on outstanding loan balance.

Source: Department of Education

Consistent with both the larger debt and the prevalence of graduate student debt among borrowers in income driven repayment, these borrowers are more likely to have completed their undergraduate degrees than borrowers in the standard repayment plan. Among those in the 2011 repayment cohort, 64 percent of borrowers in income driven repayment had completed, compared to only 48 percent of borrowers in the standard plan. Many of those who completed their undergraduate degree accumulated more debt because they subsequently enrolled in graduate school. But even among borrowers with no graduate school debt, those enrolled in an income driven repayment plan were still slightly more likely to have completed a degree.

The positive relationship between completion and income driven repayment enrollment suggests that students who enroll in income driven repayment are more likely to have large long-run returns to their college investments and to be able to eventually pay off their loans. However, data on prior repayment behavior also show that income driven repayment is being used by individuals with short-run repayment difficulties. Among borrowers entering repayment in fiscal year 2011, a sizeable fraction who enrolled in income driven repayment had experienced difficulty in repaying their loans prior to entering income driven repayment, with slightly higher signs of distress compared to borrowers under the standard plan. Over 40 percent of these borrowers had defaulted, had an unemployment or economic hardship deferment, or had a single forbearance of more than 2 months in length before entering their first income driven repayment plan. A much smaller fraction of these borrowers, roughly 10 percent, experienced difficulty in repayment after entering income driven repayment.

A key way that income driven repayment helps to improve outcomes for borrowers is by reducing monthly payments, since payment amounts are spread over a longer time period and are tied to earnings. For the 2011 repayment cohort, Figure 45 shows that borrowers in income driven repayment had lower monthly payments across all sectors, despite serving borrowers who accumulated larger amounts of debt.

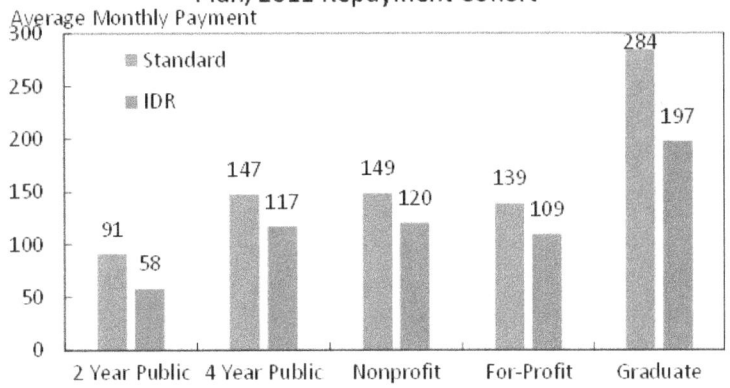

Figure 45. Average Monthly Payment by Sector and Repayment Plan, 2011 Repayment Cohort

Note: Data are for the fiscal year 2011 cohort as of fiscal year 2014. Some small sectors are excluded from this chart. Data contain some duplication across and within categories.
Source: Department of Education

As noted earlier in this report, some borrowers in income driven repayment plans may have zero dollar monthly payments. Generally, in these cases, borrowers who attended schools that did not equip them to manage their debt can stay out of default, and borrowers who are experiencing temporary periods of economic difficulty are given time to get back on their feet. Data show that the same types of borrowers who experience more difficulty repaying their loans in terms of college sector, debt size, and borrower characteristics are also more likely to have zero dollar scheduled payments, highlighting the importance of income driven repayment in helping these borrowers manage their debt. It is important to note, however, that one factor driving the large share of income driven repayment borrowers with zero dollar scheduled payments is that, on average, borrowers in income driven repayment entered repayment relatively recently. As of the end of fiscal year 2015, income driven repayment borrowers had been in repayment for an average of about three years. As Figure 6 above shows, earnings increase over a career, so as borrowers progress through their careers, their scheduled payments are also likely to increase. At the same time, as research has shown, college choice is a crucial factor—it is critical to help borrowers avoid investing in colleges that are unlikely to increase their lifetime earnings and are instead likely to leave them with high debt and low earnings. This Administration's policies have focused on strengthening college accountability and information available to students to help ensure better borrower outcomes in managing and affording debt.

In order to further expand income driven repayment to borrowers who could benefit from more manageable monthly payments, the Administration has announced a series of new actions, detailed in Box 2 below. Data about the characteristics of borrowers enrolled in income driven repayment highlight the importance of these initiatives. For example, although low balance borrowers and borrowers who did not complete are more likely to default on their loans, they represent a relatively smaller share of borrowers in income driven repayment. Enrolling more of these types of borrowers in flexible repayment plans like income driven repayment will help make their debt more manageable and help them to avoid costly and unnecessary defaults.

EXPANDING INCOME DRIVEN REPAYMENT

This April, the Administration announced a new goal to enroll two million more borrowers in plans like PAYE by leveraging key improvements in loan servicing and customer service, better tools and resources, targeted outreach to borrowers, and partnerships with key external organizations under the Student Debt Challenge. Recent actions to reach this goal include the launch of StudentLoans.gov/Repay to help drive students to their best repayment option in five steps or less, strengthening consumer protections through new standards for student loan servicing, a new set of student loan servicing disclosures developed by the Consumer Financial Protection Bureau that provides borrowers personalized information to better understand their repayment options, new work to improve the timing and content of current loan counseling efforts, a new partnership program to leverage research to drive better student outcomes, and work to develop guidance for the modernization of credit reporting. These actions will help borrowers who can benefit from flexibility in their repayment plans enroll into income driven repayment.

VII. Conclusion

College remains an excellent investment overall, and the majority of dollars in the student loan market continue to fund investments with large returns to student borrowers and the economy. However, there is variation in college quality, and particularly during the recession, many students did not receive an education that allowed them to manage the debt they incurred. At the same time, many prospective students have been dissuaded from enrolling in college because of factors like poor information, high complexity, and credit constraints. With a commitment to addressing these barriers, the Obama Administration has enacted policies to lower college costs, improve information, simplify student aid, and cap student debt at a manageable portion of borrowers' incomes.

Together these policies are a significant step forward in building a federal aid system that supports and encourages all Americans who wish to invest in an affordable, high quality college education to do so. Still, some challenges remain. First, the effectiveness of the above policies will depend on their execution, and the work started by this Administration to expand access to these beneficial programs will need to be sustained. Second, despite these efforts, many colleges still need to enhance guidance and supports to make sure that all students, especially low-income students, are able to complete an education in a field that will allow them to be financially secure. Third, work remains to continue strengthening outcomes at earlier levels of education—particularly in middle and high school, but also in the early years—to help ensure that students enter college well-prepared to benefit from their investment in higher education. Finally, policy makers will need to continue to adapt to the changing higher education landscape, which requires better data and more research to help develop new policies to better serve students. To assist in this endeavor, the Department of Education has committed to creating a process that will enable federal researchers to examine loan outcomes at a borrower level. This data will allow these researchers to build upon the analysis provided in this report to better inform policy makers and the public about student debt.

Appendix of State by State Statistics

	Student Debt Statistics by State								
	Percent 18-24 In College	2012 Cohort Default Rate	Public 2 Year Annual Tuition and Fees	Public 4 Year Annual Tuition and Fees	Total Federal Student Debt Outstanding (millions)	Number of Federal Student Loan Borrowers	Outstanding Federal Student Debt in IDR (millions)	Number of Borrowers in IDR	Scorecard Website Users
Alabama	39%	11.8%	$ 4,310	$ 9,750	$ 5,642	198,234	$ 2,264	41,952	9,960
Alaska	25%	13.0%		$ 6,570	$ 653	26,195	$ 244	4,170	2,295
Arizona	39%	14.5%	$ 2,480	$ 10,650	$ 7,761	289,254	$ 3,126	53,987	20,163
Arkansas	37%	14.5%	$ 3,400	$ 7,870	$ 3,209	126,725	$ 1,278	26,619	4,812
California	46%	11.2%	$ 1,420	$ 9,270	$ 39,971	1,361,922	$ 16,335	248,256	172,670
Colorado	40%	12.4%	$ 4,080	$ 9,750	$ 7,639	272,711	$ 3,072	52,289	25,578
Connecticut	48%	8.6%	$ 4,050	$ 11,400	$ 4,607	166,352	$ 1,456	24,819	24,289
Delaware	45%	9.3%	$ 3,570	$ 11,680	$ 1,030	37,424	$ 365	6,388	3,119
Florida	41%	14.1%	$ 3,230	$ 6,360	$ 23,918	826,525	$ 10,843	188,613	67,472
Georgia	40%	12.2%	$ 3,650	$ 8,450	$ 15,103	490,985	$ 6,308	103,715	37,129
Hawaii	36%	9.3%	$ 3,660	$ 10,170	$ 1,143	41,265	$ 425	6,799	5,332
Idaho	37%	11.2%	$ 3,870	$ 6,820	$ 2,215	86,230	$ 973	19,813	5,965
Illinois	45%	10.1%	$ 3,750	$ 13,190	$ 18,853	620,207	$ 7,361	113,645	71,481
Indiana	40%	14.7%	$ 4,320	$ 9,120	$ 9,001	345,288	$ 3,446	68,705	17,146
Iowa	45%	13.1%	$ 4,750	$ 7,880	$ 4,918	190,895	$ 1,836	33,381	9,810
Kansas	40%	9.9%	$ 2,790	$ 8,530	$ 3,909	153,789	$ 1,447	26,677	8,447
Kentucky	38%	16.3%	$ 4,650	$ 9,570	$ 5,258	205,713	$ 2,167	45,244	9,034
Louisiana	36%	11.9%	$ 3,970	$ 7,870	$ 4,767	185,870	$ 1,909	35,772	8,905
Maine	43%	10.8%	$ 3,490	$ 9,570	$ 1,799	70,423	$ 729	13,672	7,660
Maryland	45%	10.3%	$ 4,270	$ 9,160	$ 8,421	267,620	$ 3,047	44,755	30,303
Massachusetts	52%	6.4%	$ 5,620	$ 11,590	$ 9,426	330,180	$ 3,234	49,490	62,242
Michigan	45%	12.8%	$ 3,510	$ 11,990	$ 15,914	565,774	$ 6,392	112,455	35,479
Minnesota	43%	9.8%	$ 5,390	$ 10,830	$ 8,760	330,722	$ 3,173	57,612	24,790
Mississippi	41%	15.5%	$ 2,590	$ 7,150	$ 3,797	142,190	$ 1,595	31,375	3,400
Missouri	42%	11.3%	$ 3,190	$ 8,560	$ 8,578	304,823	$ 3,490	62,818	19,671
Montana	39%	9.8%	$ 3,250	$ 6,350	$ 1,233	47,556	$ 544	10,336	2,618
Nebraska	43%	8.0%	$ 2,890	$ 7,610	$ 2,478	97,426	$ 941	16,604	5,735
Nevada	32%	14.2%	$ 2,810	$ 6,670	$ 2,475	93,976	$ 1,001	17,381	6,590
New Hampshire	45%	7.4%	$ 6,510	$ 15,160	$ 2,009	74,563	$ 681	11,885	8,561
New Jersey	45%	8.2%	$ 4,600	$ 13,300	$ 11,404	409,038	$ 3,731	60,742	43,390
New Mexico	38%	20.0%	$ 1,680	$ 6,350	$ 2,026	80,132	$ 843	16,931	5,091
New York	47%	8.2%	$ 5,100	$ 7,640	$ 27,295	896,719	$ 11,122	167,891	125,159
North Carolina	41%	11.1%	$ 2,320	$ 6,970	$ 10,491	373,419	$ 4,250	77,743	35,608
North Dakota	38%	6.6%	$ 4,410	$ 7,690	$ 796	32,666	$ 298	5,468	1,794
Ohio	41%	14.6%	$ 4,530	$ 10,200	$ 19,060	687,272	$ 7,721	145,039	39,292
Oklahoma	36%	13.7%	$ 3,650	$ 7,450	$ 3,884	154,755	$ 1,520	29,654	6,901
Oregon	40%	13.7%	$ 4,670	$ 9,370	$ 6,000	205,472	$ 2,720	46,478	19,478
Pennsylvania	45%	9.7%	$ 4,930	$ 13,390	$ 18,068	631,911	$ 6,930	118,944	51,903
Rhode Island	54%	8.4%	$ 4,270	$ 11,390	$ 1,252	48,573	$ 443	7,861	6,486
South Carolina	38%	13.1%	$ 4,800	$ 11,820	$ 6,119	209,364	$ 2,650	46,430	10,151
South Dakota	36%	11.4%	$ 6,140	$ 8,050	$ 1,194	45,928	$ 464	8,682	2,295
Tennessee	38%	11.9%	$ 4,100	$ 9,260	$ 7,727	281,115	$ 3,148	58,107	17,745
Texas	37%	14.3%	$ 2,360	$ 9,120	$ 26,041	1,035,487	$ 9,323	185,834	91,592
Utah	40%	9.9%	$ 3,570	$ 6,360	$ 2,830	114,689	$ 1,215	20,927	14,302
Vermont	45%	7.6%	$ 7,530	$ 14,990	$ 913	30,170	$ 386	5,829	5,254
Virginia	43%	8.7%	$ 4,800	$ 11,820	$ 10,556	350,308	$ 3,919	62,808	49,825
Washington	36%	10.1%	$ 4,150	$ 10,290	$ 7,679	281,307	$ 3,039	51,488	36,302
West Virginia	41%	18.2%	$ 3,800	$ 7,170	$ 2,189	82,703	$ 893	17,499	3,182
Wisconsin	43%	9.2%	$ 4,470	$ 8,820	$ 7,337	293,656	$ 2,765	54,629	18,180
Wyoming	39%	13.9%	$ 2,810	$ 4,890	$ 467	19,146	$ 177	3,300	1,360

Notes: The percent in college is from 2014. The CDRs are for the 2012 cohort. College costs are for the 2015-2016 school year. Outstanding debt statistics are as of the third quarter of fiscal year 2015. Student debt data are classified by legal state of residence on last FAFSA filed. Federal student debt figures exclude commercial FFEL. Scorecard web users are as of July 14, 2016.

Source: NCES Digest of Education Statistics; Department of Education; College Board Trends in College Pricing

References

Aaronson, Daniel and Daniel Sullivan. 2001. "Growth in Worker Quality." *Economic Perspectives-Federal Reserve Bank of Chicago* 25(4): 53-74.

Abraham, Katharine and Melissa Clark. 2006. "Financial Aid and Students' College Decisions: Evidence from the District of Columbia Tuition Assistance Grant Program." *The Journal of Human Resources* 41(3): 578-610.

Altonji, Joseph G., Erica Blom, and Costas Meghir. 2012. "Heterogeneity in Human Capital Investments: High School Curriculum, College Major, and Careers." *Annual Review of Economics* 4: 185-223.

Ambrose, Brent, Larry Cordell, and Shuwei Ma. 2015. "The Impact of Student Loan Debt on Small Business Formation." Federal Reserve Bank of Philadelphia Working Paper.

Arcidiacono, Peter, V. Joseph Hotz, and Songman Kang. 2012. "Modeling College Major Choices Using Elicited Measures of Expectations and Counterfactuals." *Journal of Econometrics* 166(1): 3-16.

Avery, Christopher and Thomas Kane. 2004. "Student Perceptions of College Opportunities: The Boston COACH Program." In *College Choices: The Economics of Where to Go, When to Go, and How to Pay For It*: 355-394. Edited by Caroline M. Hoxby. University of Chicago Press.

Avery, Christopher and Sarah Turner. 2012. "Student Loans: Do College Students Borrow Too Much — Or Not Enough?" *The Journal of Economic Perspectives* 26(1): 165-192.

Bahr, Peter, Susan Dynarski, Brian Jacob, Daniel Kreisman, and Alfredo Sosa, and Mark Wiederspan. 2015. "Labor Market Returns to Community College Awards: Evidence from Michigan." CAPSEE Working Paper.

Bartik, Timothy J. and Marta Lachowska. 2013. "The Short-Term Effects of the Kalamazoo Promise Scholarship on Student Outcomes." *Research in Labor Economics* (38): 37-76.

Bartik, Timothy J., Brad Hershbein, and Marta Lachowska. 2015. "Longer-Term Effects of the Kalamazoo Promise Scholarship on College Enrollment, Persistence, and Completion. Upjohn Institute Working Paper 15-229."

Belfield, Clive, Yuen Liu, and Madeline Trimble. 2014. "The Medium-Term Labor Market Returns to Community College Awards: Evidence from North Carolina." CAPSEE Working Paper.

Bennett, William J. 1987. "Our Greedy Colleges." New York Times Opinion.

Bettinger, Eric, Bridget Terry Long, Philip Oreopoulos, and Lisa Sanbonmatsu. 2012. "The Role of Application Assistance and Information in College Decisions: Results from the H&R Block FAFSA Experiment." *The Quarterly Journal of Economics*.

Betts, John. 1996. "What Do Students Know About Wages? Evidence from a Survey of Undergraduates." *The Journal of Human Resources* 31(1): 27-56.

Bound, John, Michael Lovenheim, and Sarah Turner. 2010. "Why Have College Completion Rates Declined? An Analysis of Changing Student Preparation and Collegiate Resources." *American Economic Journal: Applied Economics* 2: 129-157.

Bricker, Jesse, Meta Brown, Simona Hannon, and Karen Pence. 2015. "How Much Student Debt is Out There?" FEDS Notes August 7. Board of Governors of the Federal Reserve System.

Brown, Meta, Sydnee Caldwell, and Sarah Sutherland. 2014. "Young Student Loan Borrowers Remained on the Sidelines of the Housing Market in 2013." Liberty Street Economics Blog March 13. Federal Reserve Bank of New York.

Brown, Meta and Sydnee Caldwell. 2014. "Young Student Loan Borrowers Retreat from Housing and Auto Markets." Liberty Street Economics Blog April 17. Federal Reserve Bank of New York.

Brown, Meta, Andrew Haughwout, Donghoon Lee, Joelle Scally, and Wilbert van der Klaauw. 2015. "Looking at Student Loan Defaults through a Larger Window." Liberty Street Economics Blog February 19. Federal Reserve Bank of New York.

Card, David. 1995. "Using Geographic Variation in College Proximity to Estimate the Return to Schooling." *Aspects of Labor Market Behaviour: Essays in Honour of John Vanderkamp.* Edited by Louis Christofides, E. Kenneth Grant, and Robert Swidinsky. University of Toronto Press.

Carnevale, Anthony, Jeff Strohl, and Michelle Melton. 2014. "What's it Worth? The Economic Value of College Majors." Georgetown Center on Education and the Workforce.

Carruthers, Celeste K. and William F. Fox. 2016. "Aid for all: College Coaching, Financial Aid, and Post-Secondary Persistence in Tennessee." *Economics of Education Review* (51): 97-112.

Casey, BJ, Rebecca Jones, and Leah Somerville. 2011. "Braking and Accelerating of the Adolescent Brain." *Journal of Research on Adolescence* 21(1): 21-33.

Cellini, Stephanie. 2012. "For-Profit Higher Education: An Assessment of Costs and Benefits." *National tax Journal* 65(1): 153-180.

Cellini, Stephanie and Latika Chaudhary. 2013. "The Labor Market Returns to a For-Profit College Education." Working Paper.

Cellini, Stephanie and Claudia Goldin. 2014. "Does Federal Student Aid Raise Tuition? New Evidence on For-Profit Colleges." *American Economic Journal: Economic Policy* 6(4): 174-206.

Cellini, Stephanie, and Nicholas Turner. 2016. "Gainfully Employed? Assessing the Employment and Earnings of For-Profit College Students Using Administrative Data." NBER Working Paper No. 22287.

Cohodes, Sarah and Joshua Goodman. 2014. "Merit Aid, College Quality and College Completion: Massachusetts' Adams Scholarship as an In-Kind Subsidy." *American Economic Journal: Applied Economics* 6(4): 251-285.

College Board. 2010. "Student Poll: Students and Parents Making Judgments about College Costs without Complete Information." *Student Poll* 8(1).

College Board. 2015a. "Trends in College Pricing: 2015." *Trends in Higher Education.*

College Board. 2015b. "Trends in Student Aid: 2015." *Trends in Higher Education.*

Committee on Health, Education, Labor, and Pensions United States Senate. 2012. "For Profit Higher Education: The Failure to Safeguard the Federal Investment and Ensure Student Success."

Consumer Finance Protection Bureau. 2012. "Private Student Loans." Report to the Senate Committee on Banking, Housing, and Urban Affairs, the Senate Committee on Health, Education, Labor, and Pensions, the House of Representatives Committee on Financial Services, and the House of Representatives Committee on Education and the Workforce.

Cooper, Daniel, and J. Christina Wang. 2014. "Student Loan Debt and Economic Outcomes." Federal Reserve Bank of Boston Current Policy Perspectives 14–7.

Council of Economic Advisers. 2014. "The Labor Force Participation Rate since 2007: Causes and Policy Implications."

Council of Economic Advisers. 2015. "Using Federal Data to Measure and Improve the Performance of U.S. Institutions of Higher Education."

Council of Economic Advisers. 2016. "The Long-Term Decline in Prime-Age Male Labor Force-Participation."

Cuhna, Flavio, James J. Heckman, and Salvador Navarro. 2005. "Separating Uncertainty from Heterogeneity in Life Cycle Earnings." NBER Working Paper No. 11024.

Curs, Bradley and Luciana Dar. 2010. "Do Institutions Respond Asymmetrically to Changes in State Need- and Merit-Based Aid?" Working Paper.

Dadgar, Mina and Madeline Trimble. 2014. Labor Market Returns to Sub-Baccalaureate Credentials: How Much Does a Community College Degree or Certificate Pay? *Educational Evaluation and Policy Analysis.*

Darolia, Rajeev, Cory Koedel, Paco Martorell, Katie Wilson and Francisco Perez-Arce. 2015. "Do Employers Prefer Workers who Attended For-Profit Colleges? Evidence from a Field Experiment." *Journal of Policy Analysis and Management* 34(4): 881–903.

Decker, Ryan, John Haltiwanger, Ron Jarmin, and Javier Miranda. 2014. "The secular decline in business dynamism in the U.S." Unpublished Manuscript: University of Maryland.

Dee, Thomas. 2004. "Are There Civic Returns to Education?" *Journal of Public Economics* 88: 1697-1720.

Deming, David J., Claudia Goldin, and Lawrence F. Katz. 2012. "The For-Profit Postsecondary School Sector: Nimble Critters or Agile Predators?" *Journal of Economic Perspectives* 276(1): 139-164.

Deming, David J., Claudia Goldin, and Lawrence F. Katz. 2013. "For-Profit Colleges." *Future of Children* 23(1): 137-163.

Deming, David J., Noam Yuchtman, Amira Abulafi, Claudia Goldin, and Lawrence F. Katz. 2014. "The Value of Postsecondary Credentials in the Labor Market: An Experimental Study." NBER Working Paper No. 20528.

Denning, Jeffrey. 2016. "College on the Cheap: Consequences of Community College Tuition Reductions." Working Paper.

Denning, Jeffrey. 2016. "Born Under a Lucky Star: Financial Aid, College Completion, Labor Supply, and Credit Constraints." Working Paper.

Desrochers, Donna and Rita Kirshstein. 2014. "Labor Intensive or Labor Expensive? Changing Staffing and Compensation Patterns in Higher Education." Delta Cost Project.

Devlin-Foltz, Sebastian and Jay Sabelhaus. 2016. "Heterogeneity in Economic Shocks and Household Spending in the US." Fiscal Studies, 37(1): 153-192.

Dominitz, Jeff and Charles F. Manski. 1996. "Eliciting Student Expectations of the Returns to Schooling." *Journal of Human Resources* 31: 1-25.

Dunlop, Erin. 2013. "What Do Stafford Loans Actually Buy You? The Effect of Stafford Loan Access on Community College Students." American Institutes for Research Working Paper.

Dynan, Karen. 2012. "Is a Household Debt Overhang Holding Back Consumption?" *Brookings Papers on Economic Activity* Spring: 299–362.

Dynarski, Susan. 2003. "Does Aid Matter? Measuring the Effect of Student Aid on College Attendance and Completion." *The American Economic Review* 93(1): 279-288.

Dynarski, Susan and Judith Scott-Clayton. 2006. "The Cost of Complexity in Federal Student Aid: Lessons from Optimal Tax Theory and Behavioral Economics." NBER Working Paper No. 12227.

Dynarski, Susan and Judith Scott-Clayton. 2016. "Tax Benefits for College Attendance." NBER Working Paper No. 22127.

Dynarski, Susan and Daniel Kreisman. 2013. "Loans for Educational Opportunity: Making Borrowing Work for Today's Students." The Hamilton Project.

Eagan, Kevin, Ellen Bara Stolzenberg, Joseph Ramirez, Melissa Aragon, Maria Ramirez Suchard, Sylvia Hurtado. 2014. "The American Freshman: National Norms Fall 2014." Cooperative Institutional Research Program at UCLA.

Ehrenberg, Ronald G. 2001. "Tuition Rising: Why Colleges Cost So Much." Forum Futures: Exploring the Future of Higher Education, 2000 Papers. Edited by Maureen Devlin and Joel Myerson.

Field, Erica. 2009. "Educational Debt Burden and Career Choice: Evidence from a Financial Aid Experiment at NYU Law School." *American Economic Journal: Applied Economics* 1(1): 1-21.

Fishman, Rachel. 2015. "2015 College Decisions Survey Part 1: Deciding to Go to College." New America Education Policy Program.

Forsythe, Eliza. 2016. "Why Don't Firms Hire Young Workers During Recessions?" Working Paper.

Goldin, Claudia and Lawrence Katz. 2008. *The Race between Education and Technology*. Harvard University Press.

Goodman, Joshua, Michael Hurwitz, and Jonathan Smith. 2015. "College Access, Initial College Choice and Degree Completion." NBER Working Paper No. 20996.

Government Accountability Office. 2010. "For-Profit Colleges: Undercover Testing Finds Colleges Encouraged Fraud and Engaged in Deceptive and Questionable Marketing Practices." Testimony Before the Committee on Health, Education, Labor, and Pensions, U.S. Senate.

Greenstone, Michael and Adam Looney. 2013. "Rising Student Debt Burdens: Factors Behind the Phenomenon." The Hamilton Project.

Griffith, Amanda and Kevin Rask. 2016. "The Effect of Institutional Expenditures on Employment Outcomes and Earnings." *Economic Inquiry*.

Grodsky, Eric and Melanie Jones. 2007. "Real and Imagined Barriers to College Entry: Perceptions of Cost." *Social Science Research* 36: 745-766.

Haskins, Ron, Julia Isaacs, and Isabel Sawhill. 2008. "Getting Ahead or Losing Ground: Economic Mobility in America." The Brookings Institution.

Heckman, James J., Lance J. Lochner, and Petra E. Todd. 2006. "Earnings Functions, Rates of Return and Treatment Effects: The Mincer Equation and Beyond." *Handbook of the Economics of Education* 1: 307-458.

Hershbein, Brad and Melissa Kearney. 2014. "Major Decisions: What Graduates Earn over their Lifetimes." The Hamilton Project.

Hoekstra, Mark. 2009. "The Effect of Attending the Flagship State University on Earnings: A Discontinuity-Based Approach." *The Review of Economics and Statistics* 91(4): 717-724.

Horn, Laura, Xianlei Chen, and Chris Chapman. 2003. "Getting Ready to Pay for College: What Students and Their Parents Know About the Cost of College Tuition and What They Are Doing to Find Out." U.S. Department of Education National Center for Education Statistics.

Houle, Jason, and Lawrence Berger. 2015. "Is Student Loan Debt Discouraging Home Buying Among Young Adults?" *Social Service Review* 89(4): 589–621.

Hoxby, Caroline and Christopher Avery. 2013. "The Missing One-Offs: The Hidden Supply of High Achieving, Low-Income Students." *Brookings Papers on Economic Activity.*

Hoxby, Caroline and Sarah Turner. 2013. "Expanding College Opportunities for High-Achieving, Low Income Students." SIEPR Discussion Paper No. 12-014.

Hoxby, Caroline and Sarah Turner. 2015. "What High-Achieving Low-Income Students Know About College." NBER Working Paper No. 20861.

Hoynes, Hilary, Douglas Miller, and Jessamyn Schaller. 2012. "Who Suffers During Recessions?" *Journal of Economic Perspectives* 36(3): 27-48.

Hurwitz, Michael and Jonathan Smith. 2016. "Student Responsiveness to Earnings Data in the College Scorecard." Working Paper.

Jacobson, Louis, Robert LaLonde, and Daniel Sullivan. 2005. "The Impact of Community College Retraining on Older Displaced Workers: Should We Teach Old Dogs New Tricks?" *Industrial and Labor Relations Review* 58(3): 398-415.

Jepsen, Christopher, Kenneth Troske, and Paul Coomes. 2012. "The Labor-Market Returns to Community College Degrees, Diplomas, and Certificates." IZA Discussion Paper No. 6902.

Kahn, Lisa B. 2010. "The Long-Term Labor Market Consequences of Graduating from College in a Bad Economy." *Labour Economics* 17: 303-316.

Kane, Thomas and Cecilia Rouse. 1993. "Labor Market Returns to Two and Four Year Colleges: Is a Credit a Credit and Do Degrees Matter?" NBER Working Paper No. 4268.

Krishnan, Karthik and Pinshuo Wang. 2015. "The Cost of Financing Education: Can Student Debt Hinder Entrepreneurship?" Northeastern University D'Amore-McKim School of Business Working Paper No. 2586378.

Kurz, Christopher and Geng Li. 2015. "How Does Student Loan Debt Affect Light Vehicle Purchases?" FEDS Notes February 2. Board of Governors of the Federal Reserve System.

Lang, Kevin and Russell Weinstein. 2013. "The Wage Effects of Not-for-Profit and For-Profit Certifications: Better Data, Somewhat Different Results." *Labour Economics* 24: 230-243.

Lavecchia, Adam, Heidi Liu, and Philip Oreopoulos. 2015. "Behavioral Economics of Education: Progress and Possibilities." IZA Discussion Paper No. 8853.

Liu, Yuen Ting and Clive Belfield. 2014. "The Labor Market Returns to For-Profit Higher Education: Evidence for Transfer Students." CAPSEE Working Paper.

Lochner, Lance and Enrico Moretti. 2004. "The Effect of Education on Crime: Evidence from Prison Inmates, Arrests, and Self-Reports." *The American Economic Review* 94(1): 155-189.

Long, Bridget Terry. 2008. "What Is Known About the Impact of Financial Aid? Implications for Policy." NCPR Working Paper.

Long, Bridget Terry. 2015. "The Financial Crisis and College Enrollment: How Have Students and Their Families Responded?" *How the Great Recession Affected Higher Education*. Edited by Jeffrey Brown and Caroline Hoxby.

Looney, Adam and Constantine Yannelis. 2015. "A Crisis in Student Loans? How Changes in the Characteristics of Borrowers and in the Institutions they Attended Contributed to Rising Loan Defaults." *Brookings Papers on Economic Activity*.

Lucca, David, Taylor Nadault, and Karen Shen. 2015. "Credit Supply and the Rise in College Tuition: Evidence from the Expansion in Federal Student Aid Programs." Federal Reserve Bank of New York Staff Report No. 733.

Luo, Mi and Simon Mongey. 2016. "Student Debt and Initial Labor Market Decisions: Wages, Job Satisfaction and Search." Working paper.

McPherson, Michael and Morton Owen Schapiro. 1999. *The Student Aid Game: Meeting Need and Rewarding Talent in American Higher Education.* Princeton University Press.

MDRC. 2016. "Using Financial Aid to Speed Degree Completion: A Look at MDRC's Research." MDRC Issue Focus.

Mezza, Alvaro and Kamila Sommer. 2015. "Predictors of Student Loan Delinquency: The Role of Borrower Credit Information." American Education and Finance Policy 40th Annual Conference, Washington.

Mezza, Alvaro, Kamila Sommer, and Shane Sherlund. 2014. "Student Loans and Homeownership Trends." FEDS Notes October 15. Board of Governors of the Federal Reserve System.

Mezza, Alvaro and Kamila Sommer. 2015. "A Trillion Dollar Question: What Predicts Student Loan Delinquencies?" Finance and Economics Discussion Series 2015-098. Board of Governors of the Federal Reserve System.

Mezza, Alvaro, Daniel Ringo, Shane Sherland, and Kamila Sommer. 2016. "On the Effect of Student Loans on Access to Homeownership." Finance and Economics Discussion Series 2016-010. Board of Governors of the Federal Reserve System.

Mian, Atif, Kamalesh Rao, and Amir Sufi. 2013. "Household Balance Sheets, Consumption, and the Economic Slump." *Quarterly Journal of Economics* 128 (4): 1687–1726.

Mitchell, Michael, Vincent Palacios, and Michael Leachman. 2014. "States Are Still Funding Higher Education Below Pre-Recession Levels." Center on Budget and Policy Priorities.

Moretti, Enrico. 2004. "Estimating the Social Return to Higher Education: Evidence from Longitudinal and Repeated Cross-Sectional Data." *Journal of Econometrics* 121: 175-212.

Oreopoulos, Philip and Kjell G. Salvanes. 2011. "Priceless: The Nonpecuniary Benefits of Schooling." *Journal of Economic Perspectives* 25(1): 159-184.

Oreopoulos, Philip, Till von Wachter, and Andrew Heisz. 2012. "Short- and Long-term Career Effects of Graduating in a Recession." *American Economic Journal: Applied Economics* 4(1): 1-29.

Ortalo-Magne, Francois, and Sven Rady. 2006. "Housing market dynamics: On the contribution of income shocks and credit constraints." *The Review of Economic Studies* 73(2): 459–485.

Ost, Ben, Weixiang Pan, and Doug Webber. 2016. "The Returns to College Persistence for Marginal Students: Regression Discontinuity Evidence from University Dismissal Policies." IZA Discussion Paper No. 9799.

Page, Lindsay and Judith Scott-Clayton. 2015. "Improving College Access in the United States: Barriers and Policy Responses." NBER Working Paper No. 21781.

Rizzo, Michael and Ronald Ehrenberg. 2004. " Resident and Nonresident Tuition and Enrollment at Flagship State Universities." *College Choices: The Economics of Where to Go, When to Go, and How to Pay For It.* Edited by Caroline Hoxby. University of Chicago Press.

Rothstein, Jesse and Cecilia Rouse. 2011. "Constrained After College: Student Loans and Early-Career Occupation Choices. *Journal of Public Economics* 95: 149-163.

Ruder, Alex and Michelle Van Noy. 2014. "The Influence of Labor Market Outcomes Data on Major Choice: Evidence from a Survey Experiment." Heldrich Center for Workforce Development.

Sahm, Claudia. 2014. "Deleveraging: Is it over and what was it?" FEDS Notes June 24. Board of Governors of the Federal Reserve System.

Stevens, Ann, Michal Kurlaender, and Michel Grosz. 2015. "Career Technical Education and Labor Market Outcomes: Evidence from California Community Colleges." NBER Working Paper No. 21137.

Singell, Larry and Joe Stone. 2007. "For Whom the Pell Tolls: Market Power, Tuition Discrimination, and the Bennett Hypothesis." *Economics of Education Review* 26(3): 285-295.

Sun, Stephen and Constantine Yannelis. 2015. "Credit Constraints and Demand for Higher Education: Evidence from Financial Deregulation." *The Review of Economics and Statistics.*

Thaler, Richard and Sendhil Mullainathan. 2008. "Behavioral Economics." The Concise Encyclopedia of Economics. Library of Economics and Liberty.

The Institute for College Access and Success. 2012. "Steps the Education Department Should Immediately Take to Curb Default Rate Manipulation."

Turner, Lesley. 2014. "The Road to Pell is Paved with Good Intentions: The Economic Incidence of Federal Student Grant Aid." Working Paper.

Turner, Lesley. 2015. "The Returns to Higher Education for Marginal Students: Evidence from Colorado Welfare Recipients." *Economics of Education Review.*

Wiederspan, Mark. 2015. "Denying Loan Access: The Student-Level Consequences When Community Colleges Opt Out of the Stafford Loan Program." CAPSEE Working Paper.

Wiswall, Matthew and Basit Zafar. 2013. "How Do College Students Respond to Public Information about Earnings?" Federal Reserve Bank of New York Staff Reports No. 516.

Wozniak, Abigail. 2010. "Are College Graduates More Responsive to Distant Labor Market Opportunities?" *Journal of Human Resources* 45(4): 944-970.

Zimmerman, Seth. 2014. "The Returns to College Admission for Academically Marginal Students." *Journal of Labor Economics* 32(4): 711-754.